Musings of a Country Vet

*I would like to dedicate this
book to my wife Patricia for being there
through the good times and the bad.*

ERIC MILLAR

Musings of a Country Vet

DRUMMOND PRESS

First published in 2005 by
Drummond Press
Kevock Road, Lasswade
Midlothian, Scotland

Text copyright © 2005 Eric Millar
Cover photograph © Paul Turner

ISBN: 0-9550465-0-5

British Library Cataloguing in Publication Data
A catalogue record for this book is available
from the British Library

Design: Mark Blackadder

Printed and bound in Livingston, Scotland
by DigiSource GB Ltd

∗
Contents
∗

*
Acknowledgements
*

I would like to thank Andrew Patterson for his invaluable help and encouragement during the initial stages of this book and for introducing me to Stephanie Wolfe Murray who took it from there to the finished copy you now hold in your hand.

I thank Paul Turner for so generously offering us a selection of photographs for the book's cover.

My thanks too to Elsa Green for typing the stories so beautifully from my impossible handwriting.

I extend my sincere thanks for the tireless support of Martin Massaro, Tessa Johnson, Frances Wood and Sandra Walker, just some of the staff at Drummond Grange Nursing Home, Lasswade,

Finally my thanks are due to Barchester Homes plc for making the publication of this book possible.

*
Foreword
*

Eric is an example to us all – cheerful, industrious and seemingly oblivious to the fact that he can barely move. To me he is a fully functioning person, making the best of what life has thrown at him.

But more than anything, he has shown me that no matter how short a time he was given to follow his great passion – being a vet – it was worth it and it has stood him in good stead for the rest of his life. And I have no doubt that for everyone who has been lucky enough to know him he has always been a cheerful, even an inspiring person to be with.

Back in the fifties it was not easy to get a place in the veterinary faculty. It was over subscribed and Veterinary Studies is a long course; five years I believe. During those years Eric had to live and there is plenty of evidence to suggest that he did just that, even finding time to get married and start a family. He then launched himself into his chosen profession with all the passion of someone who loves what he does. An eight-hour day was never for him. He was there for the farmers, and the animals, whatever the hour of the day or night. I'm sure he would insist that without the support of his wife it would have been well nigh impossible, and I would believe him.

In these stories there is plenty of evidence to show that within a very short space of time Eric's clients not only grew to respect him for his integrity, but to confide in him too. His instincts were sure and he seems to have shown a wisdom beyond his years. Considering the ground he covered on his daily rounds and the different person-alities and problems he came across, he must have had an extraordinarily wide circle of friends.

This little book only covers the years he was in practice. A lifetime has passed since it became clear that his strength was waning. You need to be physically strong to pull out reluctant calves in the middle of the night, deal with panic-stricken horses and keep everyone calm at the same time. A concerned doctor friend recommended a specialist neurologist in Sheffield who diagnosed his problem immediately: known as Charcot Marie Tooth in those days, it is now called Hereditary Motor and Sensory Neuropathy – a slow muscle degenerative disease.

Of course life didn't stop there, but that is another story. Meanwhile Eric, it is a pleasure to know you!

Stephanie Wolfe Murray

*

Beginnings

*

It is said that certain professions have a vocational nature, and veterinary medicine is certainly one of them. I had gone through the wanting-to-be an engine driver stage and moved onto being a farmer after a friend of the family took me to see his dairy farm. He gave me a pack of booklets on different aspects of farming.

Next up, my mother volunteered me to collect for the RSPCA on the North Parade promenade at Llandudno in north Wales. The friendly inspector told me all about their work and gave me leaflets.

At the age of eleven an SSPCA inspector transmogrified into a veterinary surgeon and that stayed with me although there was no influence of precedence in my family.

I went to Haileybury in Hertfordshire for my secondary education and quickly made friends with the school farm manager. He made arrangements for me to go round with the farm vet in Hertford. He just happened to be an Old Boy and had qualified at the Dick Vet College in Edinburgh. This became more than a dream for me. I was deadly serious and if it worked out, I could live in Edinburgh.

In the school holidays it was arranged for me to spend some days at a vet practice in Llanrwst, some way up the Conway River. Many of the clients had Welsh as their first language. On one of those visits the senior partner said something to me that I never forgot: 'If you go into this profession boy, you'll be closer to God than in any other profession'.

In my last year at Haileybury I won the much-coveted Corn-thewaite Natural History prize and chose as one of my books *The Black Vet Dictionary* which I had always coveted since I had first seen it at a vet's surgery. I still have it to this day.

On a visit to Edinburgh in my late teens my father took me to look round the Dick Vet college in Summerhall Square. The tour was conducted by the senior janitor, resplendent in his coat with golden crests. On our arrival in the Anatomy Dissection Room and Museum the janitor announced, 'This is the Atomy (sic) Department'. This tour couldn't have come at a better time for me. It really was a spur and I left feeling motivated and inspired.

My application failed on the first attempt so I signed up for another A Level, chemistry at Basil Paterson's College in Edinburgh. It was at this time that I met and fell in love with Patricia. Maybe she brought me luck because I passed this exam the following summer and collected my Certificate of Matriculation. But still no word from the college, so I enrolled to do a BA in Political Economy. Fresher's Week arrived and I notified my tutor that I would want to change to the Vet Course if the opportunity arose.

Then halfway through the Freshers' Conference that magic letter arrived. The Dick Vet was offering me a place. Four of us celebrated by playing golf and drinking cans of beer on Craigmillar golf course. The great journey was about to start at last, and believe me, although I only had a relatively few years to practice the profession of my choice, it was worth it. It's the journey that matters, however short. It gave me a confidence and a belief in people that has never left me.

*
First Solo Calls
*

I had married my wife when we were students. I was still on the long course to be a vet, she to be a nurse. But before we graduated she became pregnant and by the time I took up my first posting we had a three year old daughter, Carys.

We moved into our first home with me as a professional vet in Lea, near Gainsborough. The house was up a country lane and I remember it had a wonderful back garden but there was little time to enjoy it.

I spent the first five days with my fellow assistant, learning the area and meeting clients. But this pleasant state of affairs was not destined to last for long. My Irish boss decided he was off on holiday for two weeks, leaving Saturday a.m. He obviously thought we could cope and that my wife could take the phones, nights and weekends! The latter situation was an unpaid duty at first, but later I discovered I could pay my wife a certain amount per month for tax purposes.

I took my first call in the early afternoon from a pig farmer in a village over the River Trent. He had a sick pig. I set off in my Mini Traveller Estate, a fine summer's day, and went through the possible diagnoses.

I reached the farm without much trouble and donned my brown coat and put the regulation stethoscope around my neck. The farmer was a fellow Scot who had been in the RAF during the last war, stationed at one of the many aerodromes in the area. At the end of hostilities he had stayed and married a local girl. Her widowed mother lived with them too and it was obvious that they needed a man about the place, especially for the heavy work. The farmer had not been brought up on a farm but as I got to know him it was clear that he had taken to his new profession like a duck to water.

One look at the sick sow, covered in red diamond spots, I thought, 'Oh joy, it can only be one thing, Erysipelas, or pig measles. One injection of Penicillin into the neck should do the trick. Check the other pigs just in case, then some crack over a cuppa and back home'.

It was a relief to be putting all that I had learnt into practice at last and I felt confident and relaxed. I was enjoying myself!

I had seen varying methods of calving whilst 'seeing practice' with vets when I was a student. This was before the days of 'calving aids'.

My first solo calving was to a small traditional farm on the outskirts of Gainsborough, run by two brothers, one a lot older than the other.

It was a fine summer's evening as I drove up a long driveway to the yard. I was greeted by the older brother, slight of build and with bowed legs. He took me into a single stall, where a cow of indeterminate breed was tethered, but still standing. So on with the wellies and calving gown while the farmer fetched the obligatory bucket of hot water, soap and towel. Part of the head had come out, but then it had got stuck. How to get more backward force?

The farmer had a brainwave. He said, 'I know what we need lad,' and disappeared. He reappeared holding a large five foot crow bar with a point. He then thrust the bar into the broken floor. 'Sithee, we'll tie the ropes round bar and use it as a lever'. I did as he suggested and with us both bending the bar back as a fulcrum and moving back each time, a bit more calf appeared.

Then that magic moment, when the weight of the calf slid down and on to the ground, breaking the umbilical cord. A quick wipe of the mouth and nostrils with a wisp of straw — a fine female calf.

I just stood back as the calf was put with her mum. A moment to savour!

* The Long Night *

The night started with evening surgery for small animals, then back home to await the phone calls as it was my turn for night duty.

Seven p.m. My boss phoned to say that a cow was having difficulty calving. The farmer in question was one of our best clients, with a large Friesian dairy herd, so an instant response was required.

The farm wasn't far from the house and had a long made-up drive. Looking ahead I saw a lot of bright lights. 'Odd,' I thought. Then nearing the farm, a figure with a torch stepped out in front of the car.

'You can't go on. We're waiting for the vet. We're a TV company, and we're here to film a calving.'

I said 'I am the vet.'

He replied, 'I'm very sorry. I'll hitch a lift with you.' He told me that they were 'The Man Alive' team. It was a popular programme running at the time. This episode was to compare the livelihoods of three men: a Dairyman, a Postman, and a Tailor.

I kitted myself out and made for the covered yard where the cow was. The first thing that struck me was the plethora of floodlights above and at ground level. The overall effect was of clear daylight. Secondly, I noted that the whole yard was covered in fresh straw. Thirdly, the 'team' seemed to fill the yard, including a very pretty little 'continuity girl' in a mini skirt and high heels, teetering about. A thing I'd only experienced in films was the presence of the Clapperboard Boy to mark the 'takes'.

I got the calving machine ready, calving ropes into a bucket of water, then I nodded over to the Director and he signalled to the 'Clapper Boy'.

'Man Alive' 'Calving' – 'Take one'. Snap.

The cow was down, but well positioned. A cursory examination revealed that one foreleg was back, but easily straightened.

The machine was applied. It consisted of a rubber bung going flat against the cow's backside. This was attached to a long threaded hook, one on each side, to attach ropes to. The hooks were connected to a central handle to work the ratchet on the lines of a fence wire tightening system. The idea was that when the cow strained, you took the ratchet back and when she relaxed you stopped pulling.

I had plenty of help available, so with both hands I guided the head through. This is called 'the crowning'. Out came a live calf and I put it up with mum, and all the team Ooh'ed and Ah'ed.

I then gave the cow a supportive intravenous injection of Calcium 400ml. The entire exercise had taken about an hour. At this point the film ran out and the Director called out, 'Excuse me, can you do that bit again?'

Answer, 'NO.'

The programme followed months later, and the entire episode only lasted half an hour. We saw the Dairyman make the initial call and then heard him say to my boss, 'Are you coming Jim?' 'No, Eric will be.' No mention of a TV crew. Then he saw me coming into the yard with my gear and favourite tweed fishing hat that I'd been given. My bit of fame lasted about three minutes, not Andy Warhol's fifteen minutes!

I had just finished cleaning up after the calf had been put to its mum's head so she could lick her newborn when the Dairyman's wife came to say my wife was on the phone, to tell me to go to a Miss Wickens at Torksey village nearby, to another calving.

I was there in minutes and she was ready with bucket of water, soap and towel. The cow was in a field close by.

A surprise was waiting for me at the gate. There seemed to be a lot of men around the cow. Miss Wickens explained that they were her 'muscle power' who always turned out for the 'pulling'.

It was a light night but the good old Tilley lamps had been brought out. I was introduced to the village policeman, the postie, the village shop owner et al. Another Friesian, no complications, just needing a good heave.

So I produced my secret weapon – 'The Calving Machine'. The 'team' had never seen it before. We got a live calf and the men were quite content to watch.

Back at Miss Wickens' I was in her large kitchen enjoying a drink of her customary hot chocolate, the time about 11 p.m. and the phone went. It was my wife. The call was to a farm over the river at Epworth, a forty mile round trip, where a cow had put her reed bed out (uterine prolapse).

Question: Why 'reed bed'. Anything to do with Moses?

The cow had been treated for Milk Fever earlier in the day but now she was lying in an old style dairy stall and the whole 'gearbox' was lying beside her. The womb was covered in dung, and all the blood vessels were engorged, not surprising after her calving.

There's an esoteric technique for replacing the uterus in a cow. What are required are: 1. two stout helpers. 2. two large sheets. 3. a pound of sugar.

The next steps are to gently hose off the dung, then liberally apply the sugar to the surface and the blood vessels shrink. A straw bale is then placed under the cow's rear end because pushing downhill is a lot better than the opposite. Instruct your two helpers to get the womb into two sheets like a bag, one twists the ends clockwise and the other anti-clockwise.

My job was to start folding it all back in, starting at the vaginal end and as I gained ground, so the two men took up the tension by twisting the sheets.

It was going well and I was soon able to use my chest to ram the organ. Then comes that magic moment when the last bit goes in, and clenching my fist, push till the last bit falls back over the pelvic bone. An intravenous injection of Calcium C/v to help the womb contract and hopefully not prolapse again.

I drove back home and I got into bed at about three a.m. I was awakened by the dreaded phone, and guess what? The call was back to the farm I started with.

It was to a calving but no TV crew this time, which was just as well, because the Dairyman had been trying to calve her himself. By the time I got to her she was very dry in the birth canal and rapidly getting weaker.

My first examination revealed that the calf was dead, so the sooner I got it out the better. Not a happy ending this time.

I had just had time to get home and grab some breakfast, then take my daughter Carys to the village school and off to morning surgery.

The good news was that my boss was present when I arrived and pronounced that as I had hardly been to bed, I should have the rest of the day off!

✲
The Tea Party
✲

I have given this story the above title as it transported me back to a time when I was a young child just after the Second World War when afternoon tea was still the custom. I remember them with a certain amount of longing.

My first summer in practice was a very hot one and one afternoon I went to do a TB test at a small farm near my village. I had been told that a man would be looking out for me on the main road as the cattle were collected down on the marsh. My contact picked me up and off we went down a rough track to the holding pen. The twenty or so beasts were penned up and a cattle 'crush' placed at the point of the V of two wooden gates.

I put on my brown coat – no need for boots, the ground was bone dry – and my 'gun belt' with two metal holsters with gun-like syringes in each. I also had bottles of Mammalian and Avian TB in a pocket to inject, plus callipers and curved round scissors. A scribe had been volunteered to write down the ear-tag number of each beast and the two initial readings that I would take with a pair of callipers graduating in millimetres.

The beast was locked by the head in the 'crush' so that I could clip an area on the neck, pinch up the skin, measure and record, and repeat it a hand's span below the first. Finally I injected Mammalian on top and Avian below.

The test was soon over as there was plenty of manpower, all much older that me, like the owner. The farmer invited us all back for some light refreshment – his way of saying thank you.

The farmhouse was small and neat, the whitewash dazzling. Inside was equally immaculate. I was shown into a large kitchen and ushered to the sink to 'wash up'. A clean towel and a new cake of soap were provided. It was only then that I realized the long wooden table was covered in a crisp white tablecloth. On it were the best china place settings and all the milk jugs and sugar bowls were covered with muslin nets with little coloured stone weights to hold them down.

The men were all standing behind a chair waiting. The waiting mystified me till the farmer pointed to a high-backed Windsor chair with arms, inviting me to sit, which I did, and then the rest sat down.

My teacup was filled first and I got the first choice of delicious sandwiches, one of my favourite foods. I felt very moved that these good people honoured me in this way. I learned that the farmer had behaved in the same way with the previous owner of the practice and this would be the fashion in which they would treat me from now on. I always looked forward to these visits and was never disappointed.

*
Lady Godiva
*

It was a Sunday and I was on duty by myself, hoping for a quiet day. Receiving calls was the responsibility of a Vet Nurse in the Windsor Surgery. The call came to go to a horse with a cut knee at Ascot.

Now, I knew right away that a cut knee is a very difficult place to deal with. Stitching was well-nigh impossible due to lack of tissue and the skin being stretched taut over the joint. Also there was the danger of the formation of 'proud flesh' (white fibrous tissue protruding from the joint).

I once saw a good example of this when a GP had been treating a knee wound on his daughter's horse with neat Dettol!

However, I had a secret weapon up my sleeve. An old vet had told me of a secret formula from his days in the Royal Army Veterinary Corp. This involved a concentrated solution of copper sulphate splashed over the wound once a day for five days.

I arrived at the house in Ascot, in a very salubrious area. I followed a split driveway – one way to the house, and the other to the stables. I was met there by a rather butch grooms woman who went into a stable to bring out the horse. The story was that its owner had been hacking in a nearby wood when his horse stumbled in a hole and threw the rider, a retired Brigadier. The more likely tale, she said, was that the Brig, after too many post-prandial ports, fell asleep and his twenty year old mount did the same!

The knee wound on the near foreleg was indeed bad, so I handed over the concentrated copper sulphate and told her the treatment. Five days later I returned as promised. As we were walking to the stables, I heard sounds of a cantering horse. I looked to my left over a low hedge and there was a naked girl with long blonde hair riding this horse bareback. I turned to the groom and asked what was going on? She told me that the Brig. often gave permission for publicity shoots to be shot in his grounds, and this time it was 'Vogue's' turn.

Anyway, after this culture shock, the good news was that the wound had healed perfectly. You couldn't see the join! This earned me many brownie points with the Brig. who asked for me personally to check his Labrador bitch. Sadly it turned out to have mammary cancer.

The bitch was soon forgotten when I looked up and saw that the whole hall was ringed with glass cases containing dioramas of different battle scenes with model soldiers. I told him it was my hobby. So followed an afternoon of sherry drinking and looking at the rest of his collection.

He asked me if I rode, to which I had to reply, 'Very badly, sir.'

'Pity,' he said, 'I could have done with another Cavalryman.'

It turned out he was President of the Sealed Knot Society – English Civil War re-enactment.

*

Kitchen Surgery

*

A call came during evening surgery. A bitch that had been spayed that morning had burst her stitches and her guts were hanging out.

The house in question was only a hundred yards from the surgery. I was taken to a kitchen cum living-room, and there was the Labrador bitch lying on the floor with her guts wrapped in a clean white cloth.

Luckily, the owner was an ex-nurse, so that was good news as I was going to need a hand. I noticed an old lady sitting in an armchair taking a lot of notice. The owner noticed my concern and said, 'Mother, I think you should go to bed now and watch TV.'

'Oh no, dear, this is far more interesting,' and stay she did.

I asked the owner to fetch a basin of warm water with some salt dissolved in it. I then lifted all the intestines into the open abdominal cavity followed by Penicillin ointment. The wound edges were 'clean' so there was no need for debridement. I then took lengths of catgut suture taking bigger 'bites' than before as well as getting good apposition of the wound edges. The point being, that this was a mid-line incision and in a large breed such as this one, a lot more tension is put on the sutures.

Themalon had been used intravenously as a sedative. Its antidote had brought her round without incident.

I gathered that mother had enjoyed her unscheduled TV programme.

The Challenge

*

The evening surgery was just ending when I got an urgent call to go to the home of a doctor, the Senior Partner in the GP practice my wife and I had just joined in Gainsborough.

The problem was that the doctor's King Charles Spaniel had got its left hind leg caught in the curved base of a wrought iron lamp stand and was in a lot of pain. I arrived at the house on 'nob hill' and was taken into the lounge, which was expensively furnished.

The poor Spaniel was indeed caught in the 'twist'. The leg was swollen and its breathing laboured. The son of the house was holding the lamp at an angle to relieve the pressure.

The Doctor confessed that he'd been trying to anaesthetise the dog using ether and an ether mask. This was a combination doomed to failure from the start and would only further distress the patient. I got the impression that it was a case of, 'Now see what you can do'.

I injected a light dose of Themalon intravenously to sedate the dog and immediately the leg relaxed and so was released. The Doctor then mentioned that the dog had bad breath, which had not responded to mouth washes! I said I'd take a look, while the dog was lying quietly on the floor. The cause of the smell was quite obvious – rotten teeth, and they were very loose to the touch.

I always carry an old leather pouch that contained emergency surgical kit, including a pair of artery forceps. I used these to remove the offending teeth, then cleaned up the mouth. The Doctor thanked me, and his wife went to make some tea.

Maybe it was because he knew that I'd only just qualified that he gave me one final challenge. 'I'll bet you can't get the dog up and walking before you leave,' he said. Well, I was not just going to let this one go, as I carried the antidote. I injected this, then came tea, cakes and a polite chat.

Thirty minutes later I got up to go, and so did the dog, much to the assembled company's surprise. In fact it followed me right to the front door! I think the whole episode, in modern parlance, deserved a 'high five'.

*
Cruelty
*

The vet profession that I have written about so far shows the 'up side', but now I wish to deal with the 'down side', namely cruelty, death and downright neglect.

The Gainsborough practice serviced two HM Borstal Farms that the inmates worked on. I was called to the nearer of the two farms one cold winter's day, to examine a Suffolk Punch mare that had been 'maltreated'.

The farm was in the middle of nowhere, surrounded by acres of flat fields. I was taken to the stables where two magnificent Suffolk Punches were in their stalls. The Punches were a rare sight even in the sixties but more importantly they were there not for show but to work, just like any other carthorse. Harking back to another age, they had been used for ploughing and pulling old style carts and other bits of machinery.

The particular story with this horse was that of one of the boys, thinking he was alone, took a yard broom and pushed the handle up the anus of one of the tethered mares. Fortunately, another boy caught him in the act and reported it to a warden and he rang us. In the meantime, some of the lads set upon the perpetrator for his foul act. He had to be rescued by staff and locked away for his own good!

I injected the mare with Antibiotic and Cortisone, advising that she should be left in peace for the rest of the day.

It turned out that the culprit had offended before in the cruelty stakes. The last time he had taken a kitten and beaten its brains out against the wall. The senior Warden therefore had no hesitation in reporting him to the RSPCA.

The local inspector got in touch with me and asked for a written report, as he anticipated that this would lead to a court case. In due course a court date was fixed, where I was to appear as a professional witness. This was to be a daunting experience as I had never been in court before.

I sat outside the court in a passageway reading my notes, then the Usher called me. I was on! I took the stand and took the oath. The Prosecution asked me my name, profession and qualifications. Here I made my first mistake. I said that I held two degrees, BVMS and MRCVS, but quickly realized that MRCVS only referred to being a member of the Royal College of Veterinary Surgeons, having obtained the necessary BVMS (Bachelor of Veterinary Medicine and Surgery).

I quickly corrected my mistake and on we went. The prosecution led me through the sequence of events, finally asking me if the symptoms shown were consistent with physical interference and pain. I told them they were.

The defence then began to ask questions. My lingering impression of his questioning was that he made me feel that I was the one on trial, and his job was to make me question my own evidence. However, as time went on, I knew that he knew that he was onto a 'loser'.

He asked one question near the end which turned out to be a silly one. 'Mr Millar, do you not concede that if a broom handle was pushed up a mare's anus it would surely move back on the handle, thus causing more damage?'

'No Sir,' I replied, 'the mare would move forward in order to get away from the pain, but this would be hampered by the stall.'

Needless to say the case was found to be proven, but as the boy was already in custody he was removed from the farm and sent to another Borstal with an increased term to serve.

My next cruelty case centred round a man who had neglected totally his stock of poultry and rabbits.

I went with an RSPCA inspector to a smallholding near Slough.

The back garden was full of broken down hutches standing in long grass, so deep that we didn't realize at first that we were treading on the corpses of ducks in varied stages of putrefaction! The rabbit hutches contained stock that were just living, either moribund or dead, and there was no water in the bottles, no feed in the trays.

The ducks that were alive were very thin, but had managed to find some food in the grass. The case was scheduled for Court and we hoped for a life ban. The owner wasn't present when we visited but did sign over the living stock to the RSPCA later.

In court the defendant pleaded guilty, but was only fined, with the addition of a five-year ban from keeping livestock.

The last cruelty case I was involved in has happened several times since I returned to Scotland. But at this time I was still practicing in England and I was called to a sick calf at a farm some way beyond Slough.

There was indeed a sick six-month old calf. The first thing I noticed was the smell of rotting flesh. Then I saw where the smell was coming from. There were dozens of rotting carcases that dogs or rats had been eating, all stinking in a sea of mud.

The sick calf had raging pneumonia and the prognosis was poor to say the least. However, I injected it with penicillin, doubting if it would do any good or if I would ever receive payment.

I then had to warn the owner that it was the worst case of neglect I had ever seen and that I was duty bound to report the case to the RSPCA. He followed this with a lot of abuse and said that he would physically resist any further visits to the property. I rang the RSPCA and gave them the details of the case plus the threat of violence. Because of this, it was decided that a follow up visit would consist of a vet from the Ministry of Agriculture, an RSPCA Inspector, and a Police Officer.

The make up of the team was fully justified, as on arrival at the farm the farmer appeared at the locked gate hefting a shotgun. The Police Officer took charge, informing the farmer that he was in enough trouble without getting involved in firearm charges (no licence). The gun was surrendered.

The court case was open and shut. He pleaded guilty, my written evidence was accepted and corroborated. He was banned from keeping stock for life.

*
Fox Hunting
*

My own personal views on hunting the fox, deer or otter, are quite unequivocal in that I view as inhumane the pursuit of these animals by man on horseback, or on foot, with a pack of hounds. It has no place in this modern world. It is not representative of country life, and it is definitely not a sport.

The Countryside Alliance would have us believe that fox hunting helps control foxes and is welcomed by farmers. Then, realising that this just isn't true, they say that they very rarely make a 'kill'.

The fox at least has cunning in its favour, but its end at the 'kill' is often far from instantaneous, or so competent observers assure me. No, I have never been on a hunt, just as I would not go to a bullfight. I chose to be a vet to save animals from cruelty and when necessary, dispatch them humanely.

A lot of hunt people claim that they only go on the hunt to enjoy a good day's riding and to exercise their horses, adding that they are never near the 'kill', if there is one. Now I can understand this from the following experience: I was driving one early Spring in Leicestershire. It was a nice sunny morning and then I saw a fox racing down the field and cross the road into woodlands. I stopped the car and got out. I looked to my left and heard the thundering of horses' hooves, but because it was coming from 'dead' ground, behind a hill, I couldn't see anything. However I thought it must be the local hunt, sounding like an old-fashioned cavalry charge. Then followed the baying pack of hounds. It was a grand sight and sound and it showed the more attractive aspect of hunting.

I saw the downside in the damage to gates, hedges and most

importantly, livestock. If gates were left un-shut and hedges broken, stock could get out onto the roads and suffer accidents. I have had flocks of pregnant ewes running hell for leather away from the hounds causing the loss of their un-born lambs. It was the same with cows.

Hunt Masters were expected to ask permission to cross a farmer's land with the proviso that all damage would be dealt with immediately. Many of my friends and clients refused and wanted nothing to do with the hunt. Some had said yes, but after wonton damage caused by the hunt, but denied by the hunt, they said no. I saw a case of this where a client's garden hedge had a great hole in it and the flowerbeds ruined. Another farmer had delivered an ultimatum and had said, 'First time you come I'll shoot the dogs, second time the horses and third, you lot.' And they never came again!

The only time I had direct involvement with a hunt was when I took a call from a Kennel man wanting me to look at a hound, as his normal vet was unavailable. The kennels were out in the Leicestershire countryside and I could smell them before I could see them. The source of the smell soon became obvious. It was decaying flesh coming from the 'butchery' in which lay rotting carcasses of various farm animals. Such a practice gave a free service to the local farms, cutting out the expense of the Knacker man. The practice was to throw a whole or part carcass to the pack and let them get on with it.

The pack was housed in a bare concrete room with a broken floor. It was cold and damp. I examined the hound and diagnosed a mild pneumonia. I then injected it and suggested he inform his own vet.

The Kennel man asked me what I thought of his kennels. I had to tell him that I could only comment using my knowledge of inspecting boarding and greyhound kennels for a local authority and if I was inspecting his in that capacity I would have to recommend that he be closed down.

I appreciate that many people on the other side of the hunting argument see things differently. Being a lover of the countryside it saddens me to see those who care deeply about nature and farming at loggerheads about this subject.

Scotland was first to outlaw hunting with dogs to the kill. England and Wales have now followed, and for the common good say I.

*
The Fire
*

I had to put my Cortina 1300 in for a service, but the garage in Windsor promised to lend me a car for the day to do my calls. The car turned out to be a Cortina Estate that had seen better days, but they assured me it had just been serviced and was ready to go.

I transferred all my gear to the back of the estate and went off to my first call, noting that some peculiar noises were coming from under the bonnet. However, I trusted the pledges of the garage and carried on with the normal type of visits.

My last call was to a pig farm to see some pigs with breathing problems.

I drove into the farm and parked near a large wooden shed. The farmer came out from his house across from the shed, which did indeed house pigs. He managed to isolate the sick pigs into a separate pen. They were suffering from a mild respiratory infection. Not too much of a problem. I injected them, checked some others and said I would call again the next day.

I got into the car, turned the ignition key and prepared to move off when there was an almighty bang from under the bonnet, followed by smoke, then flames! I promptly leapt out of the car and called out to the farmer, who had heard the bang from the house, to phone the fire brigade.

The flames had really taken hold by this time, but I couldn't do anything about it. I decided to remove all my equipment from the back, including a new case. I took it all to what I thought was a safe place and covered it with my rubber calving gown and waders. It was then that I realized the flames were starting to singe the wooden shed, and the pigs sensed this too.

I was just explaining to the farmer that we would have to let the pigs out through the only door, near my car, in the hope they wouldn't stray far, when the fire engine roared in like the US Cavalry.

The fire had now spread to the interior of the car, but thousands of gallons of water were poured in and it was swiftly extinguished. The car was a write-off, not surprisingly. I then had to ring the surgery to say why I had been delayed and would they bring another car for me.

It was only later that the receptionist told me that she couldn't understand how calm my wife was when she phoned to say that I would be late for lunch as my car had blown up. However my wife thought she said 'a calf's blown' (bloat) quite a common occurrence, so she wasn't worried.

The following day the insurance company inspected the car and came to the amazing conclusion that the fire had been started by a cigarette (I don't smoke) lying on the back seat of the car. The garage pounced on this in an attempt to prove it was not their fault. However, when it was pointed out that the witnesses, i.e. the farmer, his family and the fire chief told it otherwise, they caved in. I believe they are still trying this sort of thing on in the hope that exasperated and busy drivers do not have the time or the power to sue the insurance companies.

A few years earlier, when we first moved to Gainsborough and my wife had to take the phone duties for the first time, the culture difference became obvious and there were a few crossed wires along similar lines such as 'to bloat' and 'blown up'. My wife was from Edinburgh and therefore spoke with a Scots accent . Trying to make sense of a Lincolnshire dialect was not easy. Not only that, but local terminology was different too.

One evening a farmer rang to say that he wanted the vet to look at a 'beast'.

My wife, having managed to get the farmer's name address and phone number, asked 'What sort of beast?'

'A beast, lass, a beast,' shouted the farmer.

'Yes but what sort of a beast, a cow, sheep or pig?'

The farmer paused, embarrassed perhaps as he was talking to a woman, then said, 'A castrated bull.'

'Oh,' said my wife, 'you mean a bullock, right. I'll give him the message.' So both parties had learnt a new word.

*

Boiled Budgie

*

One warm summer's evening in August the call came in to go to a large dairy farm near Torksey in Lincolnshire to see a pet budgie that was 'not well'.

It was my first visit to the farm, run by a father and his son. I was taken into the kitchen where a poorly looking female budgie was sitting at the bottom of the cage. She hadn't been eating or drinking and appeared to be straining, the son told me.

I picked her up and examined the cloaca and, just as I thought, I felt a hard body – an egg, stuck. The budgie was egg-bound, so I took a 2ml. syringe and needle, pierced the egg and sucked out the contents, then removed the shell. This all appeared to be a trick to the owners.

The son then asked me if there was anything they could have done themselves. I replied that there was a form of treatment that had gone into folklore, but that I couldn't recommend it. This involved holding the bird's backside over a steaming kettle but it was more likely to damage feathers and skin than the method I had used with the syringe.

The father then burst out laughing till tears streamed down his face, and all he could say was 'Boiled Budgie, Boiled Budgie'. He didn't know that a few months later his tears would be for a different reason and not for his beloved budgie.

Foot and Mouth

*

We have fairly recently come through a horrendous outbreak of Foot and Mouth. Reference was often made to the previous epidemic in 1967, a much smaller outbreak, but nonetheless a worrying and often terrible experience for those involved.

I was involved in the '67 outbreak in that our sub-county of Lindsay, north Lincolnshire, was under siege. Our job as vets and LVIs (Local Veterinary Inspectors) was to keep Foot and Mouth out, so certain safeguards were put in place. Car disinfectant dips were placed on all entry roads with a duty policeman screening visitors. Some large farms adopted this at their gates. All unnecessary visits, such as dehorning, were cancelled, or the farmer was asked if he wanted us on the premises as a lot of us had never seen F&M before. Cases of lameness and slavering at the mouth were to be carefully examined, and any sign of ulceration to be reported to the Ministry of Ag, as it was called in those days. In the meantime a 'D' notice was to be served on the farm – no stock, and no persons allowed in or out, till the official 'all clear'.

The cases were getting near our boundary. Pyres could be seen and smelt. Daily business on farms was virtually zero. We were on tenterhooks. Could we hold out and how long would it last?

The call came. Some cows were lame and slavering, and the farm was that of 'Boiled Budgie' fame!

Long faces greeted me and I was taken to the suspect cows. I hosed down the feet and had a good look. There was tissue damage and they were lame, but there were no ulcers. It could just be foot rot (an infection) or mechanical damage. The mouths too showed damage, but no weals. Now, in hindsight and in normal circumstances, I wouldn't have thought twice about a diagnosis and treatment, but these were parlous times and I didn't want to be the one to make a mistake!

I had to go in and tell the farmer that a 'D' notice would have to be served. This involved locking the gate and a temporary notice put up. The poor man was stunned, then he burst into tears. He saw a lifetime's work and his livelihood disappearing forever.

I rang the Ministry contact number and told them the position, then we had the long wait for their vet. At last he arrived and luckily he was old enough to have experienced F&M the last time round. He put on his overalls and gloves, then we examined the cows together. He described what we should be looking for.

Finally, the verdict. NOT FOOT AND MOUTH! On telling the old man the good news he burst into tears of relief. The nice thing was, they bore me no grudge and I visited them quite a lot after that.

*
Gypsies
*

Gypsies have been featured in country lore for many centuries, and I did have one or two encounters with the true Romanies, as opposed to 'travelling folk'.

One occasion was a telephone call from a phone-box concerning a horse with colic. Vague directions were given and that was it. I realized that they were just below my house on marshy ground leading to the River Trent.

It was winter, so I took the car only a certain distance down a muddy track and then stopped. I took a syringe and phial of Pethidene and the appropriate drench, then proceeded down the track on foot. I soon came upon the encampment. A line of true Romany caravans, beautifully decorated vardas (horse-drawn gypsy caravans, often with sloping roofs) and the plainest bow-topped carts were lined up on the track. I suddenly realized that my approach was being announced in English as I passed each caravan, 'The farrier's coming'. Historically, of course, farriers had been vets but in those days they were blacksmiths.

I finally arrived at an open space with a large wood bonfire burning. People clustered around it. This was not surprising, as there was a bitter wind blowing off the river. A young lad was slowly walking a Palamino round in circles. 'Good move'. I thought he was doing the right thing and that the horse was in no great distress but was a bit 'tucked up'. I injected Pethidene and explained the drench to the lad. The next task was to get payment. The lad pointed out a large female figure nearest the fire.

She was the grand matriarch of the clan and would normally have spoken Romany. However, she spoke English, accepted my diagnosis and treatment and a charge of some £2. She then delved into her voluminous chest and out of the 'bank' produced a thick wad of £1 notes. She peeled off £2 and replaced the rest and that was that.

It was only afterwards that I wondered why they had to call me in anyway. Surely herbal remedies were available?

On another occasion gypsy ingenuity and getting 'the last laugh' came at the expense of a client with a large dairy herd. For the past few years gypsies had set up camp on this farmer's land, using the wide grass verge beside the approach road. The farmer, fed up with the mess and the fact that they never asked permission, decided to take preventative action.

Knowing that the gypsies came at the same time each year, he pre-empted their arrival by filling his muck spreader and covering the verge with cow dung. By the time the gypsies arrived, the dung had dried, so they collected it all up and sold it as garden manure locally, then set up camp!

Our family had an encounter with a gypsy woman selling produce round the doors. This changed our attitude towards them. My wife answered the front door bell to a gypsy trying to sell wooden clothes pegs. She gave her spiel, but my wife was not interested and closed the door. The rest of that day everything that could go wrong did go wrong, including mysteriously exploding light bulbs! An old neighbour told my wife that she never turned a gypsy down. If she had no money she'd give her something in kind rather than close the door on her.

Ever after that, wherever we were, no gypsy was turned away. Goods were bought and fortunes were listened to. It has to be said that the house we were in was Number 13!

Poachers were just as much a part of country lore as gypsies but often more of a nuisance, especially to the local landlords. I had little experience of them, but one night in the early hours, just after seeing a pig on a farm on a disused airfield, I was torched to a halt by a police patrol car. I was told to get out and open my boot for a search. It was full of veterinary equipment of course! However, I was still asked to explain my presence. Satisfied at last, they explained the reason for the search: it was getting very near Christmas; this farm had a large flock of marketable turkeys and there had been thefts of other flocks.

Another pig farm I attended on waste-ground near the River Trent was owned by an Irishman, who had a very thick 'brogue'. In front of the broken down sties was a large notice board on a pole, and writ large upon it were the words 'NO POUCHERS' (sic). I asked him if he thought it would be effective? He just laughed and I think his reply was on the lines of 'honour among thieves'.

A well-respected sheep farmer always seemed to wear a tweed version of a Norfolk jacket, which he called his poaching jacket and in a flourish, he opened it. It was lined with many pockets of all shapes and sizes, including one he proudly told me was for the poacher – a folding 4.10 shot gun! He also had 'lurcher' dogs. Had he been a 'hobby poacher' once upon a time?

Lightening Strikes
*

Lightening has for centuries been recognised as a cause of sudden death in livestock and therefore a bane and a benison to farmers. (It could be a benison because of the insurance claim.) The object of the exercise was to convince the examining vet that 1. the beast was contiguous to a conductor, eg. wood or metal, and that 2. an electrical storm had occurred at the time of death; 3. that there were relevant scorch marks on the carcase, and 4. the beast hadn't died from any other cause e.g. anthrax, mineral deficiency, or bloat.

In my early days there were those that 'tried it on' with phrases like 'your boss would OK it' (not true)! But I would reply that without conclusive evidence, I was not putting my name to a false report.

One sudden death of a bullock in the middle of a field certainly wasn't lightening, but did look like Anthrax with dark bloody discharges from rectum and nostrils. I took two slides and spread a smear from the nostrils onto one of them. This was then stained with Methylene Blue and put in a container. I then carried out the statutory procedure. This involved closing off all of the orifices with cotton wool and telling the farmer to use strong disinfectant on the contaminated grass. The corpse was then fenced off pending an official result as it might have to be burnt in situ.

The slide was put under the microscope and on first sight there did appear to be Anthracoid type bacteria – long blue stained rods with light purple edges. My boss and fellow assistant agreed, so over to the Ministry of Agriculture Lab. After some delay the Ministry of Agriculture came down with a negative diagnosis. It was not Anthrax. Interesting!

The farmer was informed and told to have the knacker man remove the carcase immediately, and to straw burn the area where it had lain. An official eye was kept on the farm after this in case of other sudden deaths.

My most conclusive lightning case was when I made out an insurance claim for a vet — a fellow Scot — in a neighbouring practice, where the carcase had been brought to our local knacker's yard near Gainsborough. He told me that there had been a thunderstorm and 'it was lying up agin a wire fence'. It was my job to go and check that it was a genuine case.

I knew the knacker man, Mr Lord, and his son well, and true to prior instructions he had just hung the carcase up on a gimbal and left it alone. A quick glance at the shoulders showed scorch lines like three branches, technically called arborisations. I then asked for the hide to be removed and on completion these were still visible. It was a text book case with identical 'branches' on the flesh — conclusive evidence, so I was able to write a positive report.

As a postscript, I never got thanked for doing this by my compatriot, but at least he paid.

*
Combined Effort

*

One time when I was called to a calving I found a large Friesian cow that had been trying to give birth for some time without success. The cow was lying on her side in the middle of a well straw-covered yard. On first examination it was revealed that she was well dilated but getting dry, also there was a tangle of little legs. More than four! I could only feel one head but there were definitely twins wedged tight up against each other, with legs entwined. The problem was to try and extricate the calves, so that one, then the other, could be delivered.

Plenty of lubrication was needed. Luckily I'd taken a tip from a friend and carried a Fairy Liquid soap bottle around with me. It was easily applied to the anus and birth canal and a little went a long way. I told the farmer's son, a big lad, to soothe her and hold her head down to stop her getting up suddenly.

I tried for some time to untangle the twins but both were still alive and wanting out at the same time. I needed an extra pair of hands, so that the hind-most calf could be repelled whilst the other was positioned to deliver. I then had an inspired thought. What if I got the farmer to work with me, as there was enough room for two arms and time was of the essence to get live twins. I got the farmer to roll up his sleeves and 'soap up' his left arm, so that back to back in we went – he with his left arm and me with my right.

I guided his hand to the rear of the calf and told him to hold it there, while I brought the foremost calf round head first with legs in the right position. It all seemed to be working, when squeaking noises came from the far wall and I saw two furry things on the walkway.

'Bloody rats, I hate the bastards!' shouted the farmer's son. He leapt up, leaving the cow's head unattended – luckily she didn't notice. He returned with a .22 rifle, took aim and fired twice, followed by two squeals, then silence. Satisfied, he laid his rifle down and returned to his post.

In the event it was a happy ending with two healthy heifer calves, mother fine, and two dead rats.

*
Home Brews
*

The late James Herriot recounted in one of his books how he was at the receiving end of some matured home-made wine, and some very fatty home-killed bacon. I had two similar experiences.

I visited from time to time an elderly bitch poodle belonging to an equally mature couple, who lived in a large house in the village. Their daughter, in her late thirties, lived with them and could be seen riding round the village on an antique 'sit up and beg' lady's bicycle. She always seemed to look as if something or someone had greatly displeased her. Later I would find out it was someone.

The poodle had the kidney trouble that goes with old age. It was necessary for it to be treated with pills and a proprietary diet for the rest of her natural life. After a consultation, the husband would produce tea and biscuits and as he was retired he always wanted to chat.

One day, as we were having tea, the subject got round to home-made wine and the problems of producing it. I asked him if he'd ever tried it? He replied no, but that he had some bottles of beer and would I like to try one? I had to say yes, so out he went and returned with two quite large bottles and two pint glasses. It looked darkish, tasted like a Scottish Heavy and was of some potency! I soon felt very mellow, when the door opened and in came the daughter. Her eyes took in the scene and she started to mouth off about 'that's all men are good for, drinking in the middle of the afternoon', and she picked up a book and stomped out.

Her father shouted after her, 'if you had your way, all men would be castrated'. He then apologised for his daughter, but explained that this was the 'fallout' after she was jilted some years ago. My head started to spin and I was feeling rather queasy, but my glass kept filling up. I had to make the excuse that I had other calls to do and would have to go, but not before he'd pressed another bottle on me to enjoy at my leisure. I drove the short distance home and made a strong coffee.

That was my experience with home brew, but my experience with homemade food was typified by a smallholding in Lincolnshire owned by an old couple whose only stock for home use was a fat pig, traditionally killed at Christmas.

It was kept in the best of conditions and well fed, but could still get the odd 'cold'. I visited in the Autumn and the pig was fattening nicely, but had a bit of a chill so I injected it with Penicillin and told them that would do the trick, so there was no need for another visit, as costs were important to them. They were a lovely old couple steeped in country lore. They lived very simply with no mod cons and no inside toilet, just an earth closet at the bottom of the garden.

They did their own killing – I think with a heavy hammer and sharp knife. Blood collected in a large white enamel pail for black pudding, intestines for sausage skins, joints for salting and hanging, sides for curing and bacon, trotters for what they called 'faggots'. In fact every last bit was used except the 'squeak'!

I was interested to be shown the wooden slaughtering bench with two handles at each end. The husband imparted the vital piece of information that he never allowed young women at the killing in case they'd 'broken down' (menstruating), and tainted the meat!

This was not to be my last visit. I was asked to call in after the pig was killed and they'd give me something.

Now it has to be said that folk of their generation loved their fatty meat, the more the merrier, so I wasn't surprised to be handed a very greasy bundle of brown paper containing six sausages. I thanked them and left feeling rather nauseated. Back home I presented the gift to my wife, who gingerly opened the package and there were these six fat herbalised sausages already beginning to stink! We both agreed – bounteous or not – to wrap them up well again and bin them!

Farmers' wives have always been known for their baking and bread making. I have happy memories of sitting in large farmhouse kitchens with an Aga cooker heating the room and the farmer's wife covered in flour as she worked at the large, well-scrubbed pine table.

One particular lady had got it into her head that I loved her baking. This was due to a chance polite comment when we first met. In actual fact her cakes and scones were too doughy for me. I was used to my wife's excellent Scottish scones.

One day, after an early calving, Mrs Worrell cooked me a full English fry-up breakfast with a large mug of tea. I thanked her profusely, but she wasn't finished yet. Into the large, shelved larder she went and reappeared with a big plate of scones and cakes. 'Eric loves my baking, father.' (This was often how they addressed their husbands in those days in such a situation.)

Her husband shook his head in sympathy. 'Eric will be full up now.'

'Nonsense,' retorted his wife, 'young lad and just done a calving.' I was full, but not to give either of us loss of face, I ate one scone and one cake!

*
Embarrassing Moments
*

In any professional career there are times when events occur that makes you wish you were somewhere else. One such moment came whilst conducting a small animal clinic at our surgery in Corby, Northamptonshire. I should say that I had a nurse present, but she doubled as a receptionist and as the next patient was a small cat I didn't think I would need her. How wrong could I be!

In came a well-upholstered blonde with a short, blue skirt and matching tights. She told me that the cat had a bald patch on its head and on first examination it shouted 'Ringworm' to me. I got the Woods Lamp that is used to identify ringworm and put it over the patch. The expected fluorescence showed up, and that plus the alopecia and scalyness confirmed my diagnosis.

I gave her a Fulcin Cream and then advised her to wear gloves and keep the children away from the cat. Everyone should wash their hands thoroughly and burn any bedding because humans could contract Ringworm through spores getting into the skin.

No sooner had I given this caveat than the woman hitched up one side of her mini skirt, exposing a large amount of blue thigh and, low and behold, there was an angry red circular spot midway up. She was just about to peel down her tights when I stopped her saying 'No, that's OK. It's probably ringworm, you'd better see your GP as soon as possible!' She seemed satisfied, tho' I fancy she would have liked the Woods Lamp run over it.

I told the nurse the story and how near I'd been to calling for help. Anyway, she found it hilarious.

Another embarrassing moment came when there was an urgent call to a flock of sheep. It sounded like a case of acute 'Bloat' due to an excess of fresh, green grass. They needed urgent relief or else they'd die. Luckily the farm was near my village of Lea in Lincolnshire, however the sheep were in a field down on the main road to Lincoln, so I followed the farmer down.

At a gate I noticed another strange car parked and a middle-aged man standing in front of the gate. The man saw us approaching and put his hand up, 'You can't come in here,' he said.

The farmer, a bit taken aback, replied 'I think I can, it's my land!'

The poor man explained that his wife had been 'caught short' and was behind the hedge. Indeed the poor, red-faced woman had just pulled up her underwear and with tears welling up cried out, 'You won't prosecute will you?'

The farmer smiled at me and said, 'What do you think Eric? Trespassing but no damage done.' I agreed, so relief all round.

On another occasion there was a routine call to clip a budgie's beak and toenails, but this turned out to be a little unusual. I reached into the cage and caught the bird, but it is one thing to catch a budgie and another to hold onto it without crushing it!

. The budgie made a sudden bid for freedom and flew up to the window and perched out of reach. The lady owner rushed to a cupboard, grabbed a bundle of 'sticks' and said, 'Don't worry, Mister, I've got the very thing to get him down.' The sticks were in fact toy arrows with rubber suckers on the end and her ploy was to stick arrows on the wall to make perches. 'I've done this before, it always works,' she said.

Round and round they went, the bird seeming to land then flying off again till at last, by some invisible signal, the game was over, the budgie alighted and allowed itself to be caught and given into my eager, but firmer hands.

Late night calls in a country practice are not uncommon and often have to be made in darkness without the aid of street lights and white lines, always with the additional hazard that wildlife or domestic stock could suddenly appear in your headlights! However, this particular night, coming back from a call, I caught more than I bargained for in my headlights.

I came slowly round a sharp bend and there in my lights was a car, tucked into a gateway, and in the back the startled faces of a couple. The man's face rang no bells, but the woman's was familiar, recently seen from where I wondered? A fleeting moment, I thought, and I'd probably never know their true identity.

It was a few days later, whilst enjoying a mug of coffee with older members of a large local farming family who were always a mine of information, that the scene I had seen was revealed. I had just mentioned my recent encounter. Heads nodded in unison and smiles spread across weather-beaten faces.

'Oh, you'll know her lad right enough,' said one. 'He'll be the local gamekeeper, but she's a married woman, husband's badly lame, bought her Chinchillas to keep her occupied.' There then followed the final pronouncement that brooked no argument. 'Aye, she's a good looking girl, but a bit loose around the back end!' This descriptive phrase has passed into legend in our family.

Enough said. I knew immediately who they were, both clients, he with cattle and sheep, she with her Chinchilla fur farm. On my first visit to their farm, I mentioned that I had become interested in mink farms as a student, so was proudly shown her brand new charges.

I was called one hot summer's day to a private house in Old Windsor to what was logged as an 'embarrassing situation' with a male Alsation – no details given!

The door was opened by an attractive young mum in shorts and brief top. She took me into a back room and shut the door to keep the two giggling kids out and a large young Alsation in. The latter was lying down on the floor. 'He just came back like this about an hour ago but it "won't go back",' said the blushing owner.

I explained that the condition was called Para Phimosis, where the prepuce sheath had contracted on the erect penis, like a spasm, so the penis remained engorged and couldn't retract. As to the cause, I told her he'd scented a bitch 'on heat' and gone after it.

The easiest way to relieve this impasse was to get him to relax. So I injected Themalon and soon the dog was snoring and normality was restored. 'What if it happens again?' she said nervously.

'Just put some fridge ice in a towel and put it on the sheath!' I wasn't always going to be on hand.

✳
Bloat
✳

Bloat has been a known curse to farmers for centuries. It is an acute condition found in ruminates, when the large second stomach acts like a big fermenting Vat when the cow or sheep has fed on too much fresh grass or grain. The rumen would fill up with Methane gas till sufficient pressure was put on the diaphragm to impede the lungs, and if the pressure was not released, death would result. Bloat also occurs if the animal becomes 'cast', an old word for falling on its side and unable to get up.

The most dramatic individual case of Bloat that I had to attend to was when a valuable Friesian cow swallowed a potato that had stuck in its gullet, so stopping any gas escaping from the Rumen. The cow, though still standing, was in some distress and slavering a lot. I put a mouth gag in, then tried to feel for the potato at the top of the gullet. Nothing there, so it must be further down. The cow's Rumen was already swollen and precipitate action was required.

Luckily, I had heard the oft told tale about two previous assistants, who had made a name for themselves by taking the extremely risky course of operating to remove a potato from a cow, in similar circumstances, on another farm.

This is risky because you must be absolutely sure where the obstruction is, and that the cow doesn't die before completion. I took the Trocar (long, round steel knife with a sharp pointed end) and Canula (long, metal tube with two flanges at the top, each with a small hole in them), chose a point on the taught skin of the left flank and plunged the Trocar downwards, right through the Rumen. Gas was immediately released in a rush, as well as a pungent smell. The flank started to get smaller and the cow was visibly better. I then inserted a Canula into the hole and stitched it in place with strong cat gut and told the farmer to remove it in 24 hours when the potato would have passed on right down the gullet.

After the farmer had taken care of the cow, he took me inside and showed me his remarkable collection of Stone Age artefacts, all found on his land, including a lovely smooth stone, used as a skin scraper, with an indented edge to take the thumb,.

The story is also told of the vet who foolishly lit the escaping gas to show that it would burn with a blue flame. Unfortunately the flame 'blew back' like a gas jet and killed the cow!

Another time when I had to use the Canula involved a number of sheep. The scene that greeted me was straight out of Thomas Hardy's *Tess of the D'Urbervilles* where the hero shepherd is summoned to a flock that had gorged on lush, green grass. I had punctured some fifteen, too many to put Canulas in, so I just had to let the gas off and see they were upright again. I told the farmer to move them to drier pastures and 'fold' them in future with only a strip of new grass for a limited time each day.

All's well that ends well.

✲
Compassion
✲

My chosen profession had its euphoric moments, but it has its moments of pathos as well. I was called to an old cat that was constipated and not eating. The cat belonged to a teenage boy who was blind and partially paralysed. His pet was his life, his Mum told me. Her son was in a wheelchair. The cat's eyes were dirty. It was just lying on his lap and there was no response to his light stroking. I palpated the abdomen with both hands. I felt a large solid lump in the abdomen – no fur ball this, but bowel cancer and inoperable.

I broke the news to the lad, who understood right away what I was going to recommend, and he burst into uncontrollable tears. His soul mate had been condemned to death. How would his life be without him? I lifted the old cat from him, after he'd said his tearful goodbyes, and put it in a wire basket. I couldn't get out of the house quickly enough, but on the way to the car I had an idea. There was a Cat Rescue Centre quite near. If I could get a young, fit cat from there and give it to the poor lad as a replacement all might be well.

The Centre showed me a middle-aged, neutered male tabby that was quiet and gentle and would fit the bill. I borrowed a spare cage and took the cat back to the boy who was still in a terrible state. His Mum let me in and when I told her what I'd done she was thrilled.

I told him I had a surprise for him and gently lifted the cat onto his lap. Instantly he was hugging and stroking it. A sad occasion had turned into a joyous one!

*
Drunken Night Calls
*

The stress of being on night call and taking genuine emergency calls is bad enough, but these are sometimes interspersed with those that a vet could do without, namely, those where the caller has had a few units too many.

One night a slurred voice came over the phone, 'My dog's eyes are all glazed over.' After a suitable pause to come awake I replied, 'At 2 a.m. my eyes are glazed over, so I suggest that you and your dog get some sleep.' Not a terribly professional response, but a fair one in the circumstances.

Another night, a female voice came on the phone at about 1 a.m. when I had just drifted off.

'I've just got in from a party (trouble I thought) and I found my Peke lying down with his eyeballs falling out. I think he's been fighting with other dogs.' I got her name and address and told her to confine the other two dogs and keep the Peke warm and quiet.

I arrived at the Corby house to be greeted by several people in party gear. The owner of the Peke told me that she was a nurse at a local hospital. The Peke was indeed shivering with shock and both eyeballs were hanging out of their sockets. I asked for a bowl of warm water and cotton wool. These were brought and I took a wad of cotton wool, wet it, then gently pressed it against each eyeball and popped them back. My treatment seemed nothing short of miraculous to the inebriated audience, including nurse, who must have realized that she could have done this herself. I then put some eye ointment on the eyes to counter infection and an injection of Cortisone for shock. Needless to say the now sober nurse was pleased, but I declined the kind offer of a drink.

*
Uncivil Animals
*

Dogs, like people, can show unsociable tendencies, usually directed towards one particular person.

A farm I visited had two working sheepdogs who, when not working, were tied up with long chains in a darkened storeroom that I had to pass through to get to the cattle yard. The first time I went nobody had warned me about the dogs, so I got out of the car, put on my overall, waders and tweed hat and went into the storeroom. I shut the door, but instead of waiting to let my eyes become accustomed to the dim light, I moved forward too soon, for then there was a roaring growl and the two dogs launched themselves at me.

Luckily, I was almost beyond the extreme length of their chains, otherwise their combined weight would have bowled me over. Suffice to say I felt both sets of teeth go into the thigh of my right wader but not through it. I did tell the farmer, who wasn't too perturbed, joking that it must have been my hat.

However it has to be said that going into their territory, a complete stranger, with new scents, is asking to be attacked. I did visit the farm again, but this time knew the length of their chains and by now the dogs had accepted me.

A farm I visited regularly also provided nice free range (very free) eggs at a very reasonable price per dozen. The farmer also had a sheepdog that was kept in a shed when not working, just near the farmhouse.

A hint at why this was necessary became obvious if you looked at the bottom of the door. A large round hole had been chewed out of it. When a stranger came up the path, the dog launched itself at the door and bit another chunk out of it instead of the visitor. I asked Mrs Fotheringham about this habit and she just replied, 'He's a bit uncivil.'

Mrs Fotheringham was not averse to her hens pecking about in the kitchen. One day my elder daughter came with me and noticed a dead hen in a large puddle in the yard. Mrs Fotheringham's succinct explanation was 'It be drownded'.

Galloway cattle have always carried the reputation of being on the wild side and so averse to handling.

I was once called to one of the few remaining farms belonging to the Co-op. A cow had just calved but hadn't got up, so it sounded like Milk Fever. An i/v injection of Calcium Borogluconate would settle that.

The cowman led me to a partly covered yard, and there under cover was cow and calf, but warning bells sounded. She was a Galloway and wild of eye. As soon as we got near her she attempted to get up and charge. She failed, but her head followed us everywhere, her intention being to protect her calf at all costs. We waited a bit and tried again. Still no good, so I said, 'We'll go inside and have a cup of tea and wait half an hour, by which time she will be a lot weaker'. We could then put the head halter on and get her injected.

This was a risky move, but further immediate stress could push her over the edge. Half an hour later we returned. The cow was on her side and the fight gone out of her. I got the halter on and gave the life saving injection. We waited by the yard fence and after twenty minutes she was up and the calf suckling.

Miss Wickens owned a large Friesian bull called Bill. Bill weighed well over a ton and was six feet at the shoulder. He was a gentle giant, but quite a character nevertheless. While grazing on the banks of the River Trent, if he saw people walking with a dog a favourite pastime of his would be to herd them into the ruin of an old tower and hold them there till his owner came to lead him off – he obeyed her implicitly.

He was also involved in a court case in which the charge was that he'd swum the Trent and served two valuable heifers on another farm. Bill was found guilty!

My particular experience with Bill was when Miss Wickens called to say that Bill had Mastitis and was in a lot of pain. On examination this proved to be correct. One of the vestigial teats was red and swollen. I got Miss Wickens to go to his head and talk to him, whilst I stripped out the infection, then gave him a large Penicillin injection and told her to continue to strip out the teats and I would return the next day to inject him again.

Next day I arrived in the yard and called out for Miss Wickens to let her know I was ready. Big mistake. There immediately followed a loud, roaring bellow from Bill. Hearing my voice triggered this Pavlovian reaction. In his mind I was the sole cause of his pain, his owner explained, then she rushed off to pacify him. That took some ten minutes before I could re-inject him.

Ever after that incident, on all future visits, I remained silent till Miss W arrived or went straight to the house in case Bill heard my voice.

The ideal bull is one that is handled frequently, allowed to graze with cows, and if penned, has an uncovered exercise yard with bars, so that he can see what's going on. This all leads to a good temperament. A happy bull is a safe bull.

I attended a bull on one occasion that showed what can happen if these conditions are not met.

The bull was kept in a shed in almost complete darkness, as the one small window was thick with dirt. The floor was covered to quite a depth by rotting straw and dung. The bull started to bellow and paw the ground as soon as the door was opened, so I knew why several men and one with a bull pole had come with me. My eyes became accustomed to the gloom and I saw that the whole head of the bull was covered by a heavy leather mask, with a metal encircled hole near the top.

It dawned on me that the headpiece was an antique slaughtering mask, and the hole was for the gun. The bull appeared to be only able to move forward or back in a straight line, and this was because a thick wire hawser was stretched from one end of the shed to the other, and attached to the bull by the head mask. I wouldn't have thought that the bull could lie down, and I was told that the hawser was only disconnected when a cow was brought to it for service. It occurred to me that the bull could well knock its head on the roof on these occasions!

This was too much. I told the farmer that though the bull appeared all right physically, it was suffering from mental cruelty and that I could report him to the RSPCA. The farmer was contrite, but mumbled about bulls being dangerous and that's the way they'd always kept them. He didn't know what the mask was, but it had been passed on in the family. Anyway, having convinced him how much better the bull's behaviour would be, he agreed to build a proper pen and nothing more was to be said.

It is not only bulls that can be dangerous. A good example of a cow having a vicious streak, or harbouring a grudge, was shown by a Friesian cow in a large milking shed at a farm in Willingham in Lincolnshire.

She had taken a strong dislike to my boss for some reason. It should be explained that she was one of only a few horned cows in a herd and had been herd leader and bully for some time. If the herd was gathered in the yard and she sensed Jim's presence, she would barge her way through the herd making a beeline for him. She undoubtedly meant to do him serious harm, so there was only one solution – dehorning.

I carried this out using a 'crush', local anaesthetic, and a pair of 'guillotine' horn shears – no problems. The effect was immediate. She lost her place in the herd pecking order and got pushed about, so her hatred of Jim was erased.

Family Feuds

*

I was not only a country vet, I was also considered a family friend by my farm clients, and often as an arbitrator in family arguments. How had I got myself into this position, I often wondered. But I was touched by my many friendships and what seemed like people's gratitude. Some of them became family friends although we had little time for a social life, what with the girls and the endless phone calls. Besides, my wife had a social life of her own, when she had time.

A family-owned dairy farm by my village had a father, son and first cousin actively working on the farm, ably backed up by a wife and mother. The father was a skilled stockman and a strict disciplinarian and inclined to be short tempered. His wife was every bit a pillar of the village community. She was a churchgoer and also chaired the local Women's Institute. The latter organisation my wife had been persuaded to join by a neighbour.

I had noticed that the son was sweet on his cousin, but thought no more about it till one day, after complimenting his Dad on devising a simple way of using the principle of the tourniquet to raise a cow's hind leg so that I could work on the hoof, he suddenly said, 'I want to ask you something, Eric.'

I could see he was pumped up, so I said 'Yes, if I can help.'

'Well, you know that my boy is in love with his cousin?'

'Yes,' I said.

'Well I don't think it's proper. One, they're too young, two, she's a gold digger, and three, and most importantly, they're closely related, no gene pool, just like cattle. What do you think?'

I replied, 'They are indeed in love, and they are in their early twenties which is not that young. Also they are good workers and both committed to the future of the farm. The church furthermore does recognise the marriage of first cousins.' He accepted this at face value and clearly was not convinced.

The son had guessed that his father had talked to me, so when he challenged me, I said I'd work on it!

A few weeks later I arrived quite early to find a tearful son waiting for me. It transpired that earlier that morning he'd heard a gunshot from a field below the farm near the road. He ran down the road and there just behind the gate lay the bloodied body of his Dad, with his favourite Twelve Bore beside him. The ambulance was sent for, but there was no hope. The Coroner accepted the verdict of intentional suicide. I found this death very hard to come to terms with. It was my first experience of suicide but unfortunately not my last.

He was a man who appeared to have everything and no money worries to my knowledge. His temper I have already mentioned. He had been known to strike his wife. He was a perfectionist, but there must have been a darker, brooding side that finally erupted.

The good news was that the son and his cousin continued to run the farm and did eventually marry.

About this time there was a general depression in farming, especially in the pig trade, where the big farms were starting to make an impact with large contracts.

As a result the small outfits, given the slim profit margins and ever-present foreign imports, had little chance. Bank managers were the ogres, not giving much slack before pulling the rug!

I had a client with a small pig farm whose fortunes had been going from bad to worse and one day his wife asked me to have a word with her husband, who had been heard muttering to himself, 'What's it all for? What's it all about?' 'May as well end it all.' He wasn't much older than me and he too had a young family.

I found him in a wee conservatory, hunched over a wooden

table. I can't remember what I said, but I mainly listened as he poured out his troubles, the gist of which was that he felt such a failure to his family. He was the sole breadwinner, but however hard he worked nothing seemed to improve his position with the bank.

I tried to convince him that this was all down to depression and he must see his GP (something he hadn't done yet). I also told him that there was nothing wrong with his methods, but I would help him as much as I could with any tips on husbandry. The pig market was certainly depressed and the farming press portrayed a very black picture.

He did take my advice about seeing his GP and suitable anti-depressants were provided. His wife thanked me, but I told her I really hadn't done anything. However, she told me that the main thing was that he had unburdened himself to me, something he hadn't seemed able to do with anyone else and he told his wife he felt the better for it.

A good example of the almost feudal system operating on some farms presented itself when I had to go to 'cleanse' (remove the after-birth) a cow. It was a particularly smelly job and I was glad to be washing up afterwards. As I did so I heard raised voices, both male and female, so the farmer's son whom I was with rushed to the byre doorway looking rather worried and saying, 'Not again!'

The scene that met our eyes was of an older man trying to restrain a young woman from coming any further up the yard. She was shouting that she had every right to be there as she was legally his son's wife. He in turn replied that they were separated and he had banned her from ever returning to the farm. She then shouted at her estranged spouse, 'Do something, you wimp! You can't let this bastard treat me like this. It's your farm.'

The son, by his tone, was very upset and embarrassed, and apolo-gised to me and said this was an ongoing battle that had been going on for some time. I gathered it all had to do with getting the old man to let go and hand it all over to his son. I left quickly.

Forty years on I have been reading that every week a farmer takes his life and every day a farm goes out of business! I think the rot started back then, in the late sixties. Country people in villages put three professions at the top of their social tree. Their GP, their minister or priest, and their vet, of whom most would put their vet first. He would be considered as a confessor and arbitrator in family disputes.

I was acquainted with the senior member of two families running a large dairy farm, and had done them a good turn by getting a cow that had died of Bloat, rapidly into the abattoir and getting cash for half the carcase.

One day he asked me to call in to check a cow I had seen earlier. Afterwards, I went into the large kitchen for a cuppa and was surprised to find representatives of both families sitting at the long table. The two points up for discussion were the direction the farm was going and the matter of succession after the old man died or retired.

Not for the first time, I felt that I was in the invidious position of acting chairman at a very important meeting, from which any decisions made would affect the future of many. I remember there were several sensible suggestions from the young ones for diversifi-cation, but the vexed question of inheritance raised its head. I said that the family lawyer would need to be brought in.

Some things a vet cannot do.

*
Docking
*

'Docking' is usually associated with the cosmetic surgical removal of a dog's tail to conform to the Kennel Club's breed description. On the other hand it also used to apply to various breeds of horses – pretty cruel as they could use their tails to flick flies off themselves, and each other, in the hot weather.

Pigs still have their tails docked because out of boredom they are likely to eat each others' tails, even backsides. This of course is because of intensive farming. Left to themselves in a field they would have no need to resort to cannibalism. Or if they are lucky enough to be in pens, as opposed to huge concrete barns with automated feeding, give them a football and that can keep them occupied. The ideal numbers would be five a side.

I have never approved of this mutilation. The tail was put there for the purpose of giving balance and stability to the dog, and more importantly to convey signals to its owner and other dogs. How much nicer it is to see the like of a Boxer with full tail!

A silly reason for docking gun dogs like Spaniels is that their feathered tails can get caught in brambles, become infected and then have to be docked, so it might as well be done in the first place, the argument goes. I do not agree. Its legs also get caught, but they aren't cut!

Sometimes, though, I was required to dock dogs and so I had to carry a selection of copper and silver coins (pre decimal) in my pocket and a checklist in the back of my Day Diary of which coin to use with which breed.

The method we used was to place the required coin under the base of the tail with the left hand, and with a pair of large curved scissors in the right hand cut at the base of the coin and then cauterise the wound with an electric diathermy blade. No anaesthetic was used, provided the pups were no more than a few days old. I don't think they felt much, but the real trauma was in the fact that they had to be separated from the bitch and then handled by a complete stranger. The bitch could hear the pups squealing and that upset her. I noticed that the owner and breeder would deliver the pups then quickly disappear and not reappear till asked. Alright for some.

The Royal College of Veterinary Surgeons have now banned the practice, thank goodness, but there are still those who will do it at a price.

*

Trial Drugs

*

Drug companies from time to time would ask a vet to field test a drug and write a report on his findings. These drugs would usually be in the form of injections of antibiotics and anti-inflammatories.

The bulk sales and profit margins were nothing compared with human medicine sales, so the company would have to get it right the first time otherwise a lot of capital investment would be lost. The first drug I got to test drive was a pig sedative, and as we had lots of pigs in Lincolnshire it was a good area to start.

I was given a box of 25ml. vials, a book of information describing method of use and a pile of case forms to fill in. The drug was given just a letter and number at that stage. It had no name. The first case I tried it on was a young pig that had an umbilical hernia that had been left a little too long. The skin of the animal was not a good colour!

I injected the recommended dose for the pig's weight and waited. The pig was soon heavily sedated and I started to operate. The hernia sac was so friable (breaking up) that before I could reduce the hernia by gently depressing the bowel into the body cavity, I had to sew up the holes in the sac. At last I was able to put in a 'purse string' suture round the hole and pull tight.

The pig recovered eventually, but on the page for follow up comments, the farmer reported that the pig's nature appeared to change right away, going from a quiet and possibly passive pig to a very aggressive one and as a result it had put on weight faster than the others in its peer group and eventually had to be put in a pen on its own. The medication did go onto the market but I never did hear if this experience was a one off case.

Immobilon is an injectable anaesthetic both in large and small animals. It too had to be tested, because it was highly dangerous to humans. Just a scratch could lead to cessation of breathing and death if the large animal form was being used. Each box of Large Animal Anaesthetic carried a vial of the antidote to be injected immediately if accidental injection occurred.

The first animal I had to try it on was a large Hereford bull that needed its feet trimming. This was normally a labour intensive job with a squad of men with long, strong ropes to cast the bull. Imagine their surprise when I arrived in the large well-strawed box and announced that the ropes would not be needed, except to hold up the legs.

I told them that I had a new short-term anaesthetic that would allow 40 minutes to do the job, 10 minutes a foot. I took a consensus of the bull's weight, a ton and a quarter, then injected the appropriate dose. The bull finally sank down, luckily with the lower legs showing, so I decided to do these first, having the men loop a rope round each one, so that I could get at them more easily. I used a pair of hoof shears and a sharp paring knife for trimming. The thing about the large feet is that you can take large chunks of hoof off at one cut.

I was just finishing off the last hoof when the bull stirred. He was obviously coming round, so I ordered all the ropes off and everyone to stand back and as I looked at my watch it was exactly 40 minutes up. The bull seemed none the worse for the experience.

The first time I used the Small Animal version of Immobilon could hardly have been with a larger animal. It was a large, soft-as-a-brush Great Dane. It needed its dew claws removed. These are vestigial claws on the front legs that tend to catch and tear.

Prior to my visit, I had asked the owners to get him weighed, which they had managed to do. My operating theatre was the kitchen with a large table at a good height to operate on.

Immobilon was injected and the claws removed without problems and as the Dane was still snoring away Revivon was injected and a good recovery followed. The family was very pleased with the result and laughed at the amount of bandaging on each leg. I told them to keep an eye on him to see that he didn't chew at the bandaging.

Two days later they called me back. The Dane had bitten the bandages off, but the stitches were intact. The old method of dealing with this was to get a plastic bucket, cut the bottom out and place it over the dog's head and stop it getting at the stitches. It could be removed at feeding time.

However, at that time, a new commercial product had come out called an Elizabethan Frilled Collar, in different sizes and with tie-tapes that meant the flat pack collars could be bent round and tied in place. This collar did the trick for the Dane, without any bandages.

The only time a drug (the pig test anaesthetic) let me down was when a large boar needed its tusks cutting. The weight was gauged and the drug injected. We waited. And waited. But the boar showed no signs of getting sleepy, so with some misgivings I injected more. Still no result, so we had to pen him up, rope his head and wire saw the tusks off.

I had to report that for pigs over a certain weight the drug didn't work. Such comments would then be given to the drug company's rep the next time he called and I had good reason to believe that the reports were taken seriously by the manufacturers.

Going to the Dogs

*

Greyhounds are the most friendly of dogs to adults and children, but not to each other or white cats, the latter due to their likeness to the 'hares' they chase on the track.

Man has trained them to hunt and race for centuries, and my job as a vet was to ensure the continued good health and welfare of the dogs, so this would entail the supervising of British Greyhound Racing Association tracks and kennels, plus trial tracks where the dogs were kept.

The local track where I lived in Windsor was in Slough, a recognised BGRA track, where punters could not only bet, but get a good meal in a restaurant overlooking the track. There were also licensed bars.

All dogs to race on the night had to be checked in. This involved checking the animal's fitness to race, taking a urine sample to be analysed for drugs, and finally the dog had to be kennelled behind a wooden, padlocked door.

The health check involved the dog handler walking the dog up and down. The animal was then lifted onto an inspection table to get a full 'once over', head to toe. The main points to look for were high temperature, high pulse, and that all four feet – claws and pads – were up to the track.

I was criticised early on for spending too long on each dog, but being new to it I reasoned that a job was worth doing well, and as long as the dogs were in their kennels one hour before the race, why worry? One night my time spent on one dog paid off.

This was a dog that hadn't walked well, and on the table its head drooped. It had messy eyes and membranes, so I took its temperature and it was raised. I had to declare it a non-runner. Imagine my embarrassment, when over the tannoy came an announcement that 'Dog No.2 in race No.4', was declared unfit to race by the vet. There followed a loud booing and hissing by those who had lost their bets on it. A vet had the power to stop a dog racing if it was unfit and also to put a dog down on humane grounds if necessary. Broken legs and toes happened quite often after a race. The owner would be contacted to offer surgery if appropriate. However, knowing that there was no guarantee of the dog returning to its best form often they refused surgery and requested euthanasia.

Vets were not allowed to place bets, and to get somebody else to put one on was seen as bad form. However, I did find that on doing the checking out prior to the race I could make an intelligent guess as to a possible winner.

The main points to look for were that the regulation wire muzzle was on properly to stop them fighting, the 'back cloth' bearing the dog's Trap Number was buckled correctly, and lastly that the dog wasn't overheating too much. By this time the results of the urine tests would be known and obviously any positives would be withdrawn pending further enquiries.

The only time in my experience that particular care was taken over a dog's urine test was when the Kennel Steward got a phone message from New Scotland Yard to say that a dog had attracted heavy last minute betting. In the event nothing was found and the dog was unplaced.

Talking of betting, I noticed that a lot of women came to bet, and a lot of these seemed to be in an advanced state of pregnancy. They used to teeter on the edge of the stand steps. I also got to know a mother and daughter team who had bought an Irish dog, unseen, for 200 guineas. It was said to be a champion but it turned out to be nothing of the sort. The ladies just couldn't see this, or heed my advice to get rid of it. They just enjoyed a night out watching their dog race even if it came in last.

I can think of better things to do on a Saturday (and Tuesday) night than officiating at a dog track meeting. It was quite an arduous duty covering, say, eight races of 200, 400 and 880 yard distances. Each race required me to go to the kennels to check out the six dogs prior to the race. Then I had to climb a steep set of steps to the steward's box to watch the track's kennel staff in white coats put each dog into its trap.

When all was ready the 'hare' was released and allowed to race away up until a particular point when the traps opened and the race was on. The acceleration was explosive with all muscles working to full capacity. The track ran anti-clockwise in the shape of an oval and so put pressure on the left inside legs on the bends, and also as the dog was trying to run against the natural centrifugal force, fractures often occurred. You could hear a thigh bone snap from quite a distance. It was only rarely that a runner would refuse to start, and once at the finish I heard of a dog that kept on running out of the stadium, hopefully to a better life. A moral there perhaps?

At the finish, handlers had to grab their dogs to stop the fight over the 'hare' which was in fact a golden toy teddy bear skin. I then had to go down again to the kennels to check the dogs, noting any particular injuries.

One night, I had an animal with an obviously broken foreleg. It was brought into the 'surgery', a wee room with a table and a phone. The radius was indeed broken, so I had to ring the owner to give him the bad news, and to say that it could be operated on, but that it was the all important inside leg.

Needless to say, he wasn't interested. The money paid would not guarantee a successful return to racing. I had to tell him that the dog would have to be put to sleep on humane grounds.

On the whole the track was well run. On principle I never went to a 'flapping track' unlicensed by the BGRA. On these unlicensed tracks dogs had different names and aliases. Handicapping was used and dogs were moved round different tracks to get a good handicap. Licensed tracks were a great deal better for the welfare of the dogs.

Euthanasia

*

It was brought home to me in my early teens, whilst going on visits with a vet, that animals have to be 'put down' or 'put to sleep'. The first that I saw was a top Welsh Collie working on a sheep farm in the hills, but he had suddenly turned 'rogue', meaning it had taken to attacking sheep.

The sheepdog over the centuries has been trained by man to tend sheep by harnessing its atavistic pack nature to hunt, but then to stop at killing. The shepherd is the pack leader and the dog serves him and him only. The dog responds to shouted or whistled commands. A wolf pack would track a herd of deer, and be able to separate their final quarry. Sheepdogs can do this too, and use the 'eye' or hard stare, and no barking.

However, once in a while something snaps. The imparted discipline goes, and the dog moves onto the killing stage. One nip, a taste of blood, that's all it needs. Even if the damage is minimal the shepherd can't afford to keep such a dog.

In the early fifties, the drug of choice for small animals was an injection of Prussic Acid that led to a delayed and painful death. The resulting corpse was put in a sack with the neck tied and thrown into the River Conwy. By the time I was at Vet College the use of barbiturates had come in. A solution four times the normal strength used for anaesthetics was injected intravenously.

My first case of dealing with the humane killing of a large animal, as opposed to slaughter for meat, was at college. A cow that had been brought into the looseboxes for final year training purposes had become unwell. No diagnosis had been made, but it wouldn't eat, looked in pain, and got thinner and thinner by the week.

63

One morning while looking at the cow for the umpteenth time with the elderly Prof. of Medicine, I had had enough and demanded of the Prof. 'Sir, we've been looking at this cow for weeks, only coming up with the obvious notion that there is a severe bowel impaction. I would suggest that the animal be put out of its misery.'

The Prof. remained silent, then said, 'Do the rest of you agree with Eric Millar?' They did, so the cow was led to the Post Mortem Room and we followed.

'Right Mr Millar, you wanted this, so you can do the deed.' He handed me the captive-bolt gun, and showed me how to load the .22 blank cartridge that would propel the rod into the skull and brain. The gun was erroneously called the 'humane killer', when in fact it only stuns the animal temporarily, and a further process known as 'pithing' has to be carried out using a thin piece of bamboo to go through the hold made by the 'bolt', and so damaging the base of the spine.

It suddenly occurred to me that here I was acting like God, taking a life that just might have pulled through, but the cow's eyes seemed to say 'just do it'. I placed the gun at a point on the top middle of the head and pulled the trigger. One minute the cow was standing in front of me, and the next it had slumped to the floor.

It was only afterwards I realized that the Prof. had taught me a valuable lesson. Firm decisions have to be made and carried out there and then, however unpleasant.

It has often been proved that a serious accident in the middle of nowhere will attract the 'rubbernecking' of the public like flies. This premise was brought home to me one summer's afternoon near Iver in Buckinghamshire. A horse had 'spooked' in a field, and the rider was unable to control it. It leapt over a hedge to the road below. Unfortunately, just at that precise moment a car was passing and the horse landed right on top of the roof and then slithered off the bonnet onto the road.

I was well out into the countryside when I got a radio call go to a traffic accident in which a horse had been severely injured. I found a white horse writhing in agony on the road. A policeman was checking a badly dented car. The driver and the rider had been taken to hospital leaving a woman friend to wait for me.

The policeman gave me brief details, then I examined the horse. It was in extremis with broken legs, ribs and probably also a broken back. It also had difficulty breathing and a weak pulse. It would have to be humanely destroyed, but then I realised I had no gun with me as the police authority that issued a blanket cover gun licence for the practice did not approve of us carrying a gun in the car except to Horse Race Meetings. I used my radio to call the surgery but none of the vets were in, so I suggested the receptionist ring the RSPCA to ask them if they could provide a gun.

During this short period of negotiation a crowd had arrived. There were one or two cars of course, as the road was blocked both ways, but there were people on foot too. Where had they come from? How did they know? At last a car drew up and one of our RANA (Royal Animal Nursing Auxiliary) vet nurses got out carrying a box with a gun and some pellets.

'Great,' I thought. 'Now we can get on,' but then there was a setback. This gun had a facility to fire more than one type of ammunition, but how was I to adjust it to the relevant size? By this time, the horse owner's vet had arrived. He took the gun, but he too was not sure of the workings. However, after a few misfires we got the hang of it and proceeded to put the horse out of its misery.

It was always my principle to try and persuade small animal owners to say their farewells to their loved ones, and then leave the consulting room for the waiting room or home. Reasons for doing this are threefold: It's a very distressing experience (one to which I can now personally identify with); the injection may not go quite as planned; the pet, though dead, may give a passive exhalation of the lungs, then the owner will cry out 'it's not dead, you haven't done the job properly'.

The rights of owners to bury or cremate is a fair one, though the latter is very expensive. But for me, euthanasia was one of the hardest parts of veterinary medicine.

*
The Bond Connection
*

In recent months we have been able to watch again the famous early
007 films with Sean Connery as the definitive James Bond.

These early films were co-produced by Messrs Cubby Broccoli
and Harry Saltzman, though this partnership subsequently split up.
So when the call came into the Windsor Surgery to go to a horse
with colic, held in stables belonging to a Mr Saltzman, I thought
nothing of it and off I went.

The groom led me into a large loosebox, and there was a big, jet-
black stallion in some discomfort, but still on its feet. The light was
not too good for finding the neck vein to inject Pethidene, but I
need not have worried, the vein was like a hose pipe. The great beast
seemed to ease in minutes and the groom said, 'Mr Saltzman will be
very pleased, you do know who he is?'

'No,' I said, so the groom enlightened me and also informed me
that these were not his only stables because a mile or so away he built
stables especially for his pre-teenage daughter with no cost spared.

The latter fact didn't surprise me as all this area smelt of money
and many stars of the large and small screens lived here. Some time
later I was called to these other stables belonging to the the daughter
of the famous Mr Saltzman.

The sight that greeted me was straight out of a film set. There
was an open stable yard with one side taken up with boxes, these
coming to a shallow point with an archway at the apex. All had
neatly tiled roofs and brick walls. But there was something odd about
the buildings. Then I realized that everything was scaled down to
about half the normal size. In fact the design reminded me of the
large stables to be seen at Newmarket. The boxes had small ponies in

them. The tack room had small tack and everything was scrupulously clean and tidy.

A female groom of small stature came out of the office to check who I was. At the same time, a security man came round the end of the stables. My ID having been established, the groom led out a small pony with a very sore eye. On closer examination I found the upper eyelid very swollen with a messy discharge coming from it. I asked for some warm water and with wads of cotton wool cleaned the eye up.

Right enough, the lid was badly inflamed due to the condition known as Blepharitis, an infection of the hair follicles of the eyelids which caused subsequent painful swelling.

I got a tube of eye ointment from the car containing an antibiotic and a steroid to contain the inflammation. I applied a line along the eyelid and told them to apply it three times a day and I would revisit in three days.

I was hoping to meet Miss Saltzman, but was told she was far too upset to be able to look at her favourite pony. Three days later I returned to find a much improved eye and a very happy Miss Saltzman.

Eeyore

*

Donkeys have been friends to man and other animals for centuries. A kind of calming influence seems to emanate from the donkey, so often they become very much part of the family.

I was called one early Autumn evening to a private house in about an acre of land, and all sorts of pet animals, but the urgency of the call was to look at the pet donkey called Jacko. He had somehow managed to get tangled up in an old piece of barbed wire that a previous owner had left in long grass, quite unbeknown to the present occupants.

Although the light was poor, I could see that the donkey was in shock and had suffered deep cuts in the neck, head and legs. I would have to deaden the pain and deal with the shock, and then sew up the cuts. But even with lights from the house and torches, there would never be enough to see by and a method I'd used before, namely by car headlights, was not on as there was no access.

I then had a brainwave. I had noticed that the kitchen was long but narrow, so I put it to them. 'If you're willing to bring Jacko into the kitchen, where it's warm and there is good overhead lighting I think I can manage there.' A unanimous 'Yes' was the answer from the mother, father and a very tearful daughter. They said that any mess was not a problem.

Jacko was led shaking into the kitchen, and stood next to the kitchen table which held my instruments and a bowl of hot water. The father fetched a standard lamp without the shade to give extra light. I injected Cortisone for shock and while that was working I cleaned up all Jacko's wounds and injected anaesthetic. The wounds were jagged and needing debridement (trimming) to get straight edges. Jacko by this time had calmed down and had warmed up. The young girl kept him occupied at his head, so he stood stock still whilst I stitched him up. Luckily they had an outhouse with straw in to put him in for the night. I revisited Jacko a week later to take his stitches out. He looked great and all his cuts had healed and his human family were delighted.

Old School Ties

*

It was between six and seven o'clock. I had just finished evening surgery in the practice, which was located at Egham near Windsor, when I got a call to see a dog in Old Windsor which was on my way home. The house was in a very salubrious area with its own private road, which once a year was 'chained off' to the general public.

The first thing I noticed was a large Rolls Royce parked in the driveway. I learned later that the Rolls mechanic came down once a year to do a full service. Later I found out that the owner got Fortnum and Masons to deliver their famous hampers, as befits an owner of a Rolls.

I was taken into a large lounge and a fat, smooth-haired Dachshund waddled forward to greet me. However, my attention was immediately drawn to two wall crests, because they were just the same as two I had at home. One was of my old school, Haileybury, with the design of three winged hearts and an open book in the middle with the motto *Sursum Corda*. Above this were cross swords and an anchor. The other shield was that of Edinburgh University with the cross of St Andrew, a thistle, a castle and a book. It was my Alma Mater.

My client saw me look at them and asked if I recognised them. On hearing that I certainly did, he said, 'Oh, this is marvellous. It calls for a celebration!' He dived into a cabinet and produced a large decanter of sherry and two glasses. On seeing all this, I respectfully suggested that I examine the dog first, to which he readily agreed. It was a simple case of a dicky heart due to age and overweight. I produced my stethoscope and did the obligatory listening. The condition was chronic and I just repeated the script for Digitalis tablets. He poured me a large measure of what turned out to be Harvey's Cream Sherry, not sweet thank goodness. It turned out that he had been at the school some time before me but older staff that had taught him and younger ones, who'd been his contemporaries, he remembered. I was able to tell him that the school had started to take girls in the Sixth Form.

Time I noticed was getting late and I hadn't eaten for hours, so I drank up and prepared to leave. 'No,' mine host said, 'you must stay and have the other half.' The other 'half' turned out to be another full glass!

At last I was ready to go, my client saying that I must come again, which I did. I got home safely, parked the car, and went in the back door which was made up of glass panes. I then stepped onto the first stair of a short staircase and spun around to shut the door, but slipped and fell back, breaking one of the glass panes in the process. My wife came running out of the lounge wanting to know what all the noise was.

'It's alright,' I said, 'just a wee accident.' It was only then that I realized my hand was covered in blood due to little shards of glass that had cut in, some quite deeply. My wife cleaned me up with warnings not to drink on an empty stomach again.

*
Exotica
*

In the last twenty years, the keeping of pets foreign to this country has become more and more popular, but in my time as a vet they were thin on the ground. Consequently, college lectures didn't cover this, but we did have Edinburgh Zoo where we were able to gain some experience.

I first encountered an exotic pet not long after I had qualified. It was an evening surgery and a man came in with a box from which a snuffling noise was coming. He opened it up and inside was an Armadillo, which I correctly identified as a Nine Ringed Armadillo.

The poor animal was having difficulty breathing and felt very hot. I had to take its temperature, but where to put the thermometer? It seemed to be all hard shell. Eventually I found its rectum in amongst the straw-like hair. I didn't exactly know what normal was, but assumed it might be as for a cat. The result was 104.5 degrees Fahrenheit. I turned it over and listened to its chest. I heard terrible rasping breaths; obviously an acute Pneumonia.

On questioning the owner I found out that the probable cause was that the house central heating had failed and hadn't been repaired. I injected it with Penicillin, but told the owner that the diagnosis was poor. He rang me up the next day to say the poor thing had died.

I wondered then, as I do now, why anyone would want to keep an Armadillo from South America? In those days expert advice was very thin on the ground.

The exotic pet trade has escalated, leading to terrible examples of air freight abuse causing pain, suffering and death. Parrots have long been established in British homes, both for their colourful plumage, and in the case of the African Grey, their ability to mimic human speech.

One day I was called into a pub in the picturesque village of Denham not far from Windsor. The task was to clip a parrot's beak. I was taken through the bar to the living-room and there on a large wooden stand was perched an enormous South American red and green Macaw. The beak was a big black eagle-like hook with a vicious point.

I was handed a pair of padded leather gauntlets and some wire cutters. 'He isn't very keen on this procedure. He knows what's going to happen when he sees the gloves brought out,' said the publican. I thought about it for a minute and then I had it. 'We'll put a towel round him including his eyes. I'll hold his beak with my gloved left hand and shorten the overgrown beak with the cutters in my right hand.'

The parrot was swaddled in a towel and the 'hook' was cut.

'He's never been as quiet as this before. He's attacked vets before now. He must like you! Would you care for a home brewed cider?'

'Yes please,' I said.

I was taken out the back door into an apple orchard with a convenient wooden picnic table and bench. The cider was cold and certainly strong, so convivial conversation flowed. 'You know Mr Millar, we've had a well-known woman TV and singing star looking at houses here. We think it's Cilla Black.'

Indeed a year or so later, she and her family moved into a large house in the village and have remained there ever since.

The Charcoal Burner

*

I have always had an interest in the old country crafts. One night, when I had been called to see the old Springer Spaniel belonging to my doctor friend, the conversation got round to these crafts.

He asked me if I had ever seen a charcoal burner, to which I replied that I hadn't. He told me that there was an old recluse living in Laughton Wood, near Gainsborough, who did just that. At that time they were a dying breed as barbeques hadn't yet taken off.

We picked a day when we were both off duty and both our families could go for a picnic in the wood. We found a small, open glade with hot sun filtering through. There was also a man-made hollow with sand in it for the children to play in.

We had the picnic, attended by numerous flies, then the doctor, myself and the three older children went off to find our man, leaving the two wives with a young baby each.

We had gone some way into the wood when I saw an old wooden shed ahead, and in the middle of the clearing there was the charcoal kiln. An old man in a blackened raincoat and cap was pacing round the burner muttering to himself. We bid him good afternoon and asked him to explain the process.

The fuel for the kiln comes from the ancient art of coppicing. This method involves removing the smaller branches by thinning out hardwood trees like Oak and Beech and therefore encouraging new growth. The branches are cut to a similar length and these are laid in a cartwheel pattern in the kiln's base to ensure air circulation. At the centre, dry kindling and wood from the last burning that did not quite become charcoal, is stacked up.

The kiln is filled and the lid fitted. Earth is piled around the base, so that it is sealed except for small air holes. Then the kiln is lit and allowed to burn till the smoke changes to a blue colour, signifying that the fire has started to burn the charcoal. At this point, the fire is put out and the kiln allowed to cool for twenty four hours. After this the lid is removed and the charcoal removed for bagging.

The old man's past was not known precisely. Some said he was an old soldier who had never settled to civilian life. But it was wonderful to see this ancient craft actually being used. There can't have been much money in it for him. According to his friend, he was quite happy with his lot and claimed to have never had an illness in his life.

*
Steam Traction Engines
*

I have always been interested in steam engines due to two childhood experiences. The first was as a wee boy, when I was back home from a friend's house and I saw a large steam roller being loaded with coal from a pile left on a piece of waste ground near a church.

One of the two-man crew saw me gazing in awe at the monster. He smiled and said, 'Would you like to have a ride on her?'

'Yes please,' I replied.

I was lifted up next to the firebox where I was assailed by the smell of hot oil, hot metal, coal fire and tar. All was ready, so off we went up the road. The boiler was going to its next location in the town, but I lived just a few hundred yards away.

The driver spun the little steering wheel and the huge drive wheel was spinning round. I had told him my house name, 'Elvaston', and sure enough he stopped the roller right outside. I thanked him and was lifted down, and it was only when I got outside that I realized I had tar on my hands. Panic, it'll never come off, I thought. But my mother worked on them with butter wrapping papers and pumice stone.

The second experience was at about the same time. A treat on a Sunday afternoon was to walk to a nearby railway bridge to watch the trains passing underneath. This day, the driver of an engine called up to us. 'Do you want to come for a ride with me?' My father replied that we certainly would. So down we went, and once again I was hoisted up into the cab of the seemingly living breathing engine.

I was shown the inside of the firebox, and off we went. My father held me up so that I could see ahead out of one of the windows. The driver took the engine, no carriages or trucks behind, about a mile up the track between two golf courses. He then reversed back to where we had started from. For a final treat, he took the engine onto the turntable and his fireman took us right round.

The steam traction engines were in their heyday before and after the Second World War, but into the fifties farming methods were changing. Diesel or petrol fuelled tractors were needed to cope with larger fields. Manpower was greatly reduced due to the migration to the cities. Combine Harvesters came from America in response to these changing conditions.

By the sixties, when I was a new vet, the steam traction engines had had their day. I was therefore pleased when I first arrived in Lincolnshire to find that some of these engines were still alive and working. It was a veritable time warp.

An early call in my new practice took me to a yard and there, gleaming in the sunlight, were two engines, lovingly restored and looking as good as new. The farmer told me that he took them to the Traction Engine Shows of which there were still many in the country.

At these shows the engines were lined up in rows according to size and usage. The biggest were the fairground engines that generated the power for the showground rides and lights and they had simulated brass bands with old fashioned figurines. These engines were very colourfully decorated with the showman's name on the side of the roof. Steamrollers and traction engines proudly displayed their maker's name, such as 'Marshalls', a local firm in Gainsborough.

Races between the engines would follow, sometimes round an obstacle course. There was much pulling of whistles and shouted encouragement and clouds of steam.

However, the real interest to me was the engines that were still working. I have mentioned before that horses were still used for ploughing, but rarer still were the Cable Ploughing Traction Engines, working in pairs. One engine was placed at one end of the field, and one at the other, each with a large drum underneath with a stout cable wound on to it. This was attached to a plough, so that one engine pulled the plough across, then the other, directly opposite, pulled it back along a new furrow. So both engines progressed forwards at right angles to the furrows. This was still a slow method and was only used for small fields. Nevertheless it was a joy to watch.

I had given up ever seeing what was perhaps the epitome of the work done by a traction engine. This was the powering of the old fashioned wooden threshing machine. The old farmers had told me about the good old days when a threshing machine towed by a steam engine would move round the villages.

I was therefore over the moon when I espied white smoke above the hedgerows, apparently moving towards me. Round the bend came a large traction engine pulling a large orange-red threshing machine. Behind it was a small hut to carry coal and spare bands for the threshing machine. I stopped the car in order to watch the whole 'train' sweep into an open gateway. I knew the farmer so I asked if I could watch and naturally he agreed.

Plenty of willing hands had come up from the village to help, as well as numerous children and dogs, the latter hoping to chase rabbits and rats disturbed by the work.

The big drive band was attached to the drums on the steam engine and thresher. Sheaves of corn were fed into the top of the machine and the cycle started. I was soon aware of a thick, dusty yellow cloud, with the sunrays piercing through, surrounding this rural scene, one that soon would be seen no more. *Sic Transit Gloria Mundi.*

The value of these engines to their owners was put in perspective when I went into the kitchen of the first owner I visited. His wife told me that if it came down to a choice between her and the two engines, she would have to go!

To this day enthusiasts still cherish these machines, so perhaps not *Sic Transit* ... yet!

*
Lambing
*

My favourite time of the year in practice was that period from just before Christmas drifting on to March. The exact date depended on the breed of sheep as to when each annual lambing took place. A large Suffolk flock I went to in Lincolnshire would usually guarantee a pre-Christmas lamb, sometimes even on the day itself.

I have memories of going to this farm at night having come from another lambing, getting out my rubber parturition gown only to find it frozen after washing it at the last farm. There was nothing for it but to put it on and try to thaw it with the hot water provided.

The ewes due to lamb were penned up in an open yard which was very cold to work in, but as soon as they had lambed they were put into a covered strawed shed in single pens with their lambs. Luckily I had learned some tricks of lambing years before.

The first thing was to check at what stage the ewe was stuck at by vaginal examination. If for instance the cervix hadn't dilated properly an injection of calcium would help this quite quickly, but if it had dilated and the lamb was too big to deliver normally then a Caesarian would be indicated.

Usually, a head or legs would have appeared at the vulva, but come no further. A bale of straw and some loose straw having been obtained, the ewe was tipped up so that her back end rested at an angle up on the straw bale, while the head and neck lay on the straw. The idea of this was that downward pressure from my hand and arm could be exerted on the lambs to push everything back into the uterus and start again.

In other words, I could sort out which head belonged to which legs, then line up the first head and forelegs to bring it out in the normal 'diving' position. A full breech presentation, that is, coming backwards with hind legs tucked right back, can be repelled and straightened out using plenty of lubrication and hands rather than ropes. I had a slim wrist, so this made it easier to work inside the womb.

When the lamb was delivered, the first thing to do was to clear the mouth and nostrils, and clean the body with straw. A wisp of straw was then poked up the nostril to get it breathing and this was followed by a slap on the back just like a human baby.

I have heard of farmers and vets swinging the lamb round and round above their heads, but there is the danger of that terrible moment when the lamb slips out of the hand and flies into oblivion. I deem this practice totally unnecessary.

Sometimes if a lamb did not respond to the above techniques for stimulating breathing I perfected a First Aid method.

One day I was called to a lambing flock owned by a coal merchant. It wasn't just one lambing, but several ewes were in trouble. They were penned in a field up a hill in a corner where it was freezing. The ewes had been trying to give birth for some time. Their owner, having other interests as well, had just taken a look as he happened to be passing.

The first lamb didn't respond to the usual stimuli to breathe, so I thought I'd give it one more chance to come into the world. I picked it up and held its mouth up to mine, and puffed short breaths into the lamb. Nothing happened at first and I thought my grand act had failed, then suddenly the lamb coughed and the lungs started to work. I had applied this mouth to mouth method with another two lambs with the same success. The owner was overjoyed and thanked me profusely.

This act of First Aid was spread around the area and my fame grew. Also farmers learned it was something they could do themselves.

Nature has given the ewe just two teats, but as the demand upon agriculture has grown for more and more, faster and faster, by the time I was in practice triplets had started to appear regularly, soon to be followed by quads. This was a problem.

Alexander Graham Bell perhaps had this in mind when having invented the telephone, iron lung and the hydroplane, he became interested in sheep and lambing. Noting that the ewe had only two teats, he embarked on a breeding programme to double the teats. He chose a breed with long teats and crossed them with established breeds. Unfortunately farmers took exception to Bell messing about with their established bloodlines, so his well-intentioned experiment foundered.

The Aga cooker has been around for many years and has graced many a farmhouse kitchen. One use that the makers didn't think of was that the ovens would be used as intensive care units for 'cade' lambs, wrapped in towels. These were newly born lambs that, for whatever reason, had been abandoned by the mother. Frequent causes were triplets, death of a mother or the lamb too cold and weak to suckle, or simply the ewe showed no interest.

Another fairly common practice, if a mother sheep had died giving birth, was to allow a healthy mother who had lost a newborn lamb to 'adopt' the orphan. In order for her to accept a lamb that was not her own, we would cut the coat off the dead lamb, fix it over the orphaned one, and hey presto! the new mother accepted it as her own.

The farmer's wife would be responsible for these lambs and the consequent bottle feeding around the clock. Unfortunately some might not have had that all-important suck of Colostrum, the first milk containing antibodies but the success rate was really impressive thanks to the gentle heat of the Aga's lower oven and the personal attention and coddling given by the family.

The word 'Cade' or 'Kaid' is used throughout the country. As to its origin I can only guess that it might come from the Latin verb 'Cedo', to fall, although even Chambers Dictionary doesn't seem to know its origin.

If a Caesarean had to be done, three straw bales were needed – two for a table and one for instruments. The ewe was put on her side and wool was removed from the area of the flank. The area was scrubbed and the skin and muscles were infiltrated with local anaesthetic. A vertical line was cut down the abdomen. The womb was brought to the outside and the lamb, or lambs removed and the mother sewn up.

A lasting memory of lambing at the first farm I mentioned with the Suffolks was a call for me to get home a.s.a.p, as my wife needed to go to the cottage hospital to give birth to our second daughter! We called her Heather and she beat me to it. I missed the actual birth but I am happy to report that there were no complications.

Traditionally, after a successful lambing, the vet and the shepherd partook of a celebratory nip of whisky. Cheers!

The Queen's Visit

*

The vet practice in Windsor was honoured to attend to the cattle and sheep belonging to the Queen in Windsor Home Park, and the livestock in Windsor Great Park, the latter being Crown Property. The Home Park had a marvellous Victorian dairy with all its original, illustrated tiles and bowls.

One time, when the Queen was up in Scotland, some of the Corgis were left behind in the charge of the Head Keeper, who just happened to be the father of the shepherd whom I knew well. He told me that one of the Corgis had been involved in a fight with one of the gun dogs, and come off worst. As a result the left hind foot had become infected.

Antibiotic was administered and the foot wounds were cleaned and bandaged. The dog was kept in the practice kennels so that the foot could be 'plotted' in hot water and re-dressed each day.

Time went on and the foot didn't seem to be getting any better, in fact the infection started to creep up the leg. The only course was for a senior partner to inform the Queen that an amputation would be necessary to save the dog's life. She agreed to this and the operation was carried out successfully and the dog kept in to recuperate. The Castle rang to say that the Queen had expressed a wish to come and see the dog for herself, so a date and time was arranged for her to visit.

The impending visit triggered the usual knee jerk response. Everywhere must be cleaned and tidied. All ordure must be removed from walls; no time for painting, but all rooms were to smell sweetly.

The morning of her visit arrived and all was ready. I think I was expecting a huge chauffer driven car, but in fact a rather ordinary

Ford Cortina Estate drove into the yard, driven by the Queen herself. She was right on the dot as always, and she was dressed just in a jacket, trousers and a headscarf. She was accompanied by a single plain clothes' man sitting in the passenger seat. He jumped out smartly, putting up a large umbrella as it was pouring down.

We were lined up to be introduced to her with the instructions to bow, only speak when spoken to and to address her firstly as Your Majesty, then Ma'am (to rhyme with Spam). The introductions were soon over and the Queen proceeded to the consulting room.

It just happened that particular weekend that my in-laws were down to stay from Edinburgh and my father-in-law brought with him a copy of the *Scottish Sunday Express*. One of the front-page headlines was 'Queen not pleased with operation on Corgi'.

The article claimed that the queen had been informed that the amputation would be below the knee, but when she saw that it had been done above the knee she was not well pleased. Unfortunately I did not carry out the operation but had I done so I am certain I would have made the same decision. This story never appeared in the English press and I never found out who leaked it to the *Scottish Sunday Express*.

Although we often went to the Royal Home Farm to tend to the animals, we rarely met actual members of the royal family, so this incident was unusual. However I did meet Princess Anne up at Windsor Great Park to see a horse that belonged to one of her friends whose father was the Head Steward of the park. The horse was very sick indeed but I was able to diagnose the problem as being Fistulous Withers. I had to fit in a draining wad from the top to the bottom of the fistula and inject it with antibiotics of course.

The princess was concerned and helpful. She seemed to have a very practical streak and she struck me as being more male than female, but pleasant nevertheless. Her friend told me that she continued to ask after the horse for many months.

The Windsor practice was not all about royal animals. It was an area my wife and I had never particularly wanted to live in. Film stars, nannies and their charges often came into our surgery. We felt we were country bumpkins and were very happy to be just that. We left there with no regrets.